No L... the
Ultimate Sales Tool

To Frank –
All the Best,

[signature]

4/1/05

No Lie—Truth Is the Ultimate Sales Tool

Barry Maher

McGraw-Hill

New York   Chicago   San Francisco   Lisbon   London
Madrid   Mexico City   Milan   New Delhi   San Juan
Seoul   Singapore   Sydney   Toronto

The McGraw-Hill Companies

Library of Congress Cataloging-in-Publication Data

Maher, Barry.
    No lie—truth is the ultimate sales tool / by Barry Maher.
        p.   cm.
    Includes bibliographical references and index.
        ISBN 0-07-141104-6 (alk. paper)
        1. Selling.   2. Sales promotion.   3. Marketing.   I. Title.
    HF5438.25.M324   2003
    658.85—dc21

                                                2003010122

1 2 3 4 5 6 7 8 9 0   DOC/DOC   0 9 8 7 6 5 4 3

ISBN: 0-07-141104-6

This publication is designed to provide accurate and authoritative information in regard to the subject matter covered. It is sold with the understanding that neither the author nor the publisher is engaged in rendering legal, accounting, or other professional service. If legal advice or other expert assistance is required, the services of a competent professional person should be sought.
                    —*From a declaration of principles jointly adopted by a committee*
                        of the American Bar Association and a committee of publishers

This book is printed on recycled, acid-free paper containing a minimum of 50% recycled de-inked fiber.

McGraw-Hill books are available at special quantity discounts to use as premiums and sales promotions, or for use in corporate training programs. For more information, please write to the Director of Special Sales, Professional Publishing, McGraw-Hill, Two Penn Plaza, New York, NY 10121-2298. Or contact your local bookstore.

To Rosie, my ultimate truth.

Contents

v

Preface

Turning Negatives into Selling Points

No Lie—Truth Is the Ultimate Sales Tool. You might think this is a book about ethics.

It's not.

I'm a big fan of ethics. When I sell, I sell according to my ethical standards. When you sell, I assume you sell according to your ethical standards. I'm happy for both of us. But that has nothing to do with this book. This is a book about sales techniques that work. It's about simple, easy-to-use techniques that build instant trust and credibility and can help you sell more whether you're a highly experienced sales professional, a novice sales rep, or a complete nonsales type who needs help selling your products and services or even yourself, your vision, and your ideas.

The key word here is *instant,* as in instant trust, because these techniques will help you sell more, right now, today. If they didn't, no one would use them. It's all well and good to talk about honesty and ethics in selling and about selling with full disclosure and building long-term trust and credibility to generate more sales down the road. But no sales manager wants to hear, "I didn't make my numbers, but I'm building valuable relationships." Salespeople need more sales now. They need to make a paycheck and feed their families.

Do salespeople care about honesty and ethics? Of course they do. Like almost everyone else on the planet, they want to feel good about what they're doing in their careers and their lives. They want to be honest with their customers; they want to be honest with themselves. They want to be able to sell with full disclosure. But they need to be able to sell—and sell today, not just sometime in the vague future. They need to be able to generate instant trust and credibility. They need to be able to tell—and *sell*—the truth the first time they ever call on a customer. That's what this book is all about.

The anecdotes, examples, stories, case studies, parables, and pontifications packed into these pages represent most of what I've learned in a lifetime of selling and working with salespeople. Remember that if sometime down the road I try to sell you a sequel.

Dancing Skeletons

No Lie—Truth Is the Ultimate Sales Tool is based on one extraordinarily simple premise: Every product, every service has its potential negatives. Great salespeople aren't afraid of those negatives. They don't stumble over them, and they certainly don't try to hide them. Great salespeople use potential negatives as selling points; they even brag about them.

As George Bernard Shaw said, "If you cannot get rid of the family skeleton, you might as well make it dance."

Truth is the ultimate sales tool.

Acknowledgments

More people have helped create this book than I can possibly thank. But let me begin with those who have shared their experiences and their truths with me over the years, sometimes even at risk to their careers. Still, if you think you recognize someone in these pages in a situation that may put his or her career at risk, you're mistaken. Whenever necessary, names have been changed and situations have been disguised.

I'd also like to thank Barry Neville, editor extraordinaire, and all the people at McGraw-Hill. Barry was the prime mover behind *No Lie—Truth Is the Ultimate Sales Tool.* Without his insight, encouragement, and sense of humor, this would be a far different book. And without the generosity of my agent, Andrew Stuart of the Stuart Agency, it probably wouldn't be a book at all.

Barry Maher
Las Vegas, NV/Helendale, CA
www.barrymaher.com

1

Making the Skeleton Dance

The company sold consulting services. That morning I'd met with some of their less successful reps. Most of them knew exactly why they weren't selling. "Our prices are just too damn high," they assured me repeatedly. I'd heard it before. Price is often the single biggest objection, the single biggest potential negative that salespeople have to deal with.

Now I was riding with Helen Daniels, the woman who'd been at the top of the company's national sales report for the last 3 years running. We were meeting with the VP of operations of a good size uniform company. Sure enough, when the issue of price came up, the VP acted exactly as those reps had predicted, using almost the exact same words they'd used.

"Sounds to me like you people are awful damn expensive," he said accusingly.

"Absolutely," Helen agreed, offering her brightest smile.

"So why do you charge so much?"

"Simple," she said. "Because we can!"

"What?"

"We charge that much because we can—because our clients are not just willing but happy to pay those kinds of rates for the results we generate."

"But can't they find someone else to do the job for less?"

"Absolutely."

"Somebody who will do the exact same job for less?"

"Well, they could certainly find companies that will charge less. I'm no expert on the kind of work these people might do, so I really can't say whether or not they'll do the exact same job."

"So you're saying, 'You get what you pay for'?"

"No," she smiled, "I'm saying to get us, you've got to pay for us. I really don't know that much about the kind of work these other companies do. Or why they charge less. Maybe you should ask them. I don't know a lot of businesses that charge less if they could charge more, but maybe they're humanitarians."

"I seriously doubt that," the VP said.

"Well, like I say, I'm no authority on their work. We charge more because our clients are happy to pay more for the results we generate. Maybe these other companies charge less because that's what *their* clients are willing to pay for the results *they* generate."

"But *your* rates . . . ?"

"Expensive."

"*Very* expensive."

"Exactly. And worth every penny. And let me tell you why," which she then proceeded to do.

That's *making the skeleton dance.* Helen took the potential negative of price and bragged about it so hard that she not only made that skeleton dance, she made it polka. Twenty-five minutes later, we walked out of there with a signed contract.

You and the Perfect Product

Truth: You may have no need for this book.

Perhaps your products and services are perfect; perhaps there's nothing negative that anyone can say about them. Perhaps competitive reps pack up their samples in despair and slink out the door at the mention of your company's name. Perhaps the first seven people you contact tomorrow morning will interrupt your initial interest-creating remark to tell you they've been waiting for a call like yours because they desperately need a huge order of your most expensive, highest commission product. Perhaps. Stranger things have happened. Not in my lifetime, but I suppose they have happened.

Of course, if your products and services were perfect, you wouldn't have a job, would you? A perfect product wouldn't need a salesperson, just an order taker.

Truth: Your products are not perfect.

As a salesperson, you know that better than anyone else. Your customers constantly remind you of current imperfections. From time to time, they stumble upon new ones. Prospects pick your presentations apart for the slightest signs of potential negatives. Anything they miss . . . Well, maybe that's why God created that army of competing salespeople: to help keep you honest. (Just like mosquitoes, bubonic plague, brussels sprouts, and political commercials, there has to be some reason for their existence.)

Hiding the Rotting Rhino

So your products are not perfect. That's why your company had to recruit and train someone like you to sell them rather than just hiring someone at minimum wage to go out and fill up bushel baskets with stacks and stacks of orders. But for you to be able to sell those products, you've got to deal with those imperfections, those potential negatives, in every call you make. Now there are any number of ways that salespeople try to deal with potential negatives, and some are more successful than others. Before we try to make your particular skeletons dance, let's take a quick look at some of the classically unsuccessful strategies that salespeople frequently resort to when confronted by potential negatives in their products and services.

The first I call *hiding the rotting rhino*. If there's (somehow) a rotting rhinoceros in the well that provides the drinking water of that country estate the sales rep is trying to sell (it could happen), he'll do everything in his power to see that the buyers don't discover that unsettling little detail until after the deal is closed and his commission check is cashed. Aside from the ethics involved, hidden rhinos are like embarrassing relatives: They seldom remain hidden for long. So this is not a strategy that generates repeat business and long-term customers. It is, however, the perfect strategy if you're planning on leaving town right after the sale, you're never planning to return, and you have no conscience.

Because of these rather obvious drawbacks, until recently major corporations seldom actively embraced the hidden rhino strategy, though management sometimes looked the other way when it was used, hoping to ensure the sales force reached its quotas. Today, however, with such massive pressure to make short-term goals and with long-term thinking less and less lucrative for corporate leaders, even some of the world's best-known companies are hiding some pretty big rhinoceri.

Long-distance telephone companies may have led the way. The hidden charges in their "low-rate" calling plans are legendary and growing by the moment. My own long-distance calls are handled by a telecommunications giant that shall remain nameless. Suffice it to say that their initials are AT&T. Last month, I was trying to call one of my vendors. But every time I dialed the number, I got a recorded message: "Sorry, your call cannot be completed at this time. Please try again later." This went on for hours. Since I was calling New Hampshire, I assumed it was a rural area, and maybe the string had broken between a couple of the tin cans or perhaps survivalists had cut the lines. Still this is the twenty-first century even in much of New Hampshire, and I figured that 5 or 6 hours should be more than sufficient to complete a phone call. Eventually, I dialed the operator. For her, the call went through immediately. Unfortunately, by that time the office I was calling had closed.

A few weeks later, I got my phone bill. The charge for the 1-minute operator-assisted call, which actually must have been considerably less than 1 minute, was $10.88! Plus tax.

Now I have no doubt that the operator's time is worth $652.80 per hour ($10.88 per minute × 60 minutes). At least it is to her. And I'm sure AT&T is paying her close to that. But it wasn't as if I'd used her assistance because I was too lazy or too incompetent to dial the call myself. I'd had to go to her because the service I was paying AT&T for wasn't working.

Since phone bills are more difficult to decipher than the average CIA code, I normally would never even have caught this type of charge. But I got lucky this time, so I complained about it. At least I did after I finally stumbled through their audio-text labyrinth (suggested motto: We raise our productivity by lowering yours) and unearthed a human being, a customer service rep.

The rep's tone was that of a kiddie-show hose—an exasperated, long-suffering kiddie-show host. "You did," he sighed, "have the option of continuing to try the call yourself. That would have cost you nothing."

Somehow this failed to appease me. It wasn't the money, you understand. It was the prin . . . No, come to think of it, it was the money.

But almost immediately he said, "Well, I can lower this charge for you. I'll give you a credit."

I accepted the credit of course. But from a customer service standpoint, offering the credit was almost worse than the original charge. It was like admitting it wasn't justified, because he wasn't saying, "The charge was a mistake. I'm sorry. We try not to make mistakes, but when we do, we fix them." It seemed more like, "We're trying our best to screw you, but since you were vigilant enough to catch us, we'll make it right."

How much has AT&T spent over the years trying to build consumer trust? And of course they're hardly the only major company that seems to have adopted this type of hidden rhino practice recently. Today, the strategy for many corporations appears to be, "When customers uncover the rotting rhinos, maybe they'll simply assume the competition is as sleazy as we are, and they won't bother to take their business elsewhere." Or maybe it's, "Let's just do whatever we can to make our goals for this quarter. Maybe we can cash in our stock options and get out before the backlash hits."

Tapping the Land Mine

Another classically unsuccessful strategy that some salespeople use for dealing with potential negatives, is *tapping the land mine*. A land-mine tapper sees every potential negative as a deadly explosive. But her ethics, her company, or necessity requires that she disclose the horrible thing to the prospect, and that means at least tapping the ground where the land mine is buried, even though she's terrified that it's going to blow up in her face.

The tapping often goes something like this: "I just need you to initial a couple of these clauses on the contract. It's mostly just boilerplate legalese. This first clause guarantees delivery in 10 days or less. The second one simply gives the price: $897 per month, just as we agreed. This third line is your color selection. Sunrise yellow, right? This next clause here makes us your only supplier in perpetuity. Oh, and this section down here is the full parts and labor warranty. It's the best in the industry, believe me. Good for a full 120 days. *What?* No, I said, *in perpetuity*. But look at this warranty. Isn't that something? It's good for 120 days come hell or high water, come feast or famine. Parts *and* labor. *What?* No, just us. In perpetuity. But isn't this a great warranty! And it's going be yellow! Sunrise yellow. Isn't that just glori . . . *What?*"

Treat a negative like a land mine, and when you do tap, you virtually guarantee an explosion.

Mealy-Mouthing

The most common unsuccessful strategy for dealing with potential negatives is probably *mealy-mouthing.* Think of Helen Daniels, that top consulting company rep I discussed at the beginning of the chapter. ("Why do we charge so much? Because we can!") A mealy-mouther is the exact opposite of Helen. And the week after I worked with Helen, I ran into her opposite—on the same issue, price.

The woman was gorgeous, and she was waiting for me as I came off the stage after making the keynote presentation to an association of sales executives. While I answered questions for other attendees, she stood at the edge of the crowd, smiling—seductively, I thought—whenever I looked over. She reminded me of Michelle Pfeiffer, only more so. Whatever her product or service might be, I was ready to buy one on the spot—possibly two.

Once I finished talking to the others, she approached, her face lighting up. She said, "I'd like to discuss hiring you to consult with our sales force."

"Damn," I said, "I was hoping you were some kind of a sales training groupie."

"Sales training groupie?"

"I didn't say there were a lot of them."

She told me she was the CEO of a premium industrial machine company. She had a number of problems with her sales team, and she thought I might be able to help. "But the biggest issue, first and foremost," she said, "is that we have a lot of low-cost competitors, and our salespeople are getting killed trying to deal with the problem of price."

She looked at me as if she expected me to remedy the situation right then and there. When I just stared back, she invited me to lunch. We went to an overpriced restaurant in the hotel lobby called Viva Zapatos!

"I think they mean Viva *Zapata*, the Mexican hero," she explained. "Viva *Zapatos* means *long live shoes!*" We ordered anyway. Over $18.00 worth of watery tostada, I looked through her product catalogs.

"I can see why you're having a problem with price," I said.

"You can?"

"Certainly. Your machines are too expensive."

She looked shocked. "They are?"

"Aren't they?"

"I don't know. I don't think so."

"Is that what you tell customers?" I asked. "That you don't think they're too expensive?"

"No. Of course not."

"So what would you tell me if I were a prospect and I said that I thought your skimming machine here on page 25 was too much money?"

"I'd say, *No*. No, it's really not all that expensive."

"Go on."

"I mean, it's not that expensive. Not really. Not when you understand that our patented skimmers are working for you 24 hours a day, 7 days a week, 365 days a year. Or at least they're capable of that. So if you do the math, it's really less than 93 cents a minute, and when you amortize that over the effective life of the machinery and figure in the potential long-term savings in quality control, not to mention the benefits in morale and subsequent increases in operator productivity and the possibility of at least slightly increased customer satisfaction, then put all that together and it comes to less than . . . blah, blah, blah"

Blah.

She sounded like she was trying to convince herself. She could have been twice as beautiful, and the spiel wouldn't have persuaded anyone else. And since it was obviously a canned recitation of the company line, I could imagine that her salespeople sounded just as lame. It was a timid, semiapologetic effort to prove that black is white and that a lot of money was not really a lot of money. And I could see that when this type of mealy-mouthing didn't work, her salespeople might just be tempted to forget to mention the additional shipping charges or the costly downtime necessary for installation. When I asked her if those types of omissions were sometimes a problem, she nodded.

What I mean by mealy-mouthing is stumbling around the potential negative, apologetically explaining—make that over-explaining—and ensuring that the negative becomes the focal point of the entire presentation. The more the rep goes on, the more importance the negative takes on in the mind of the prospect. It doesn't take long before the mealy-mouther starts sounding like a 3-year-old explaining that he wasn't the one who took the cookies. Not him. Really. Never mind the crumbs all over his chin and shirt and the chocolate chip smears on his fingers.

This CEO's sales reps were afraid of the cost of their own products. I can't think of a better way to frighten away potential customers.

The Small Con

One of the oldest strategies for dealing with potential product negatives is *the big con*: getting prospects to buy by conning them into it, by misrepresenting the terms of the deal, or simply by failing to deliver what was promised. These are the people who get exposed by Mike Wallace or Morley Safer on TV and then have the chutzpa to feature "As Seen on *60 Minutes*" in all their advertising.

Some of them are notorious. There are home improvement scam artists who prey on the elderly after hurricanes. There are fund raisers for groups with familiar sounding names, but virtually none of the money raised goes to those it's supposedly intended to help. There are used car dealers who resell totaled cars that have been doctored or who crank back odometers to make everything old seem new again. But those who practice the big con aren't salespeople by any stretch of the imagination; they're criminals.

Unfortunately, though, there *are* sales organizations that practice *the small con*. They call us up and pretend we've won some type of prize or trip. They offer guarantees with enough undisclosed strings to build a macramé skyscraper. Their hidden charges turn what sounds like a good deal into something uncomfortably close to a swindle. When sleazy telemarketers do this kind of thing, it's called fraud. And the government, occasionally at least, prosecutes them. Reputable organizations, of course, never resort to the small con.

Of course not. And I know something about dealing with reputable organizations, believe me. In fact I recently received a message on my voice mail informing me that I had just been nominated to serve on the Republican Presidential Committee. Would I please call their toll-free number immediately? When I called and asked who had nominated me, the woman who took the call told me that the nomination had come from the Republican Congressional Committee. And I didn't even realize those people knew that I was alive.

"So who on the committee nominated me?" I wondered.

The woman wasn't sure. She did know that the committee thought it would be invaluable if a key business leader like me would lend his name and agree to serve.

"You know I never thought of myself as a key business leader," I said.

"Well, that's the way we think of you here."

Wow.

She explained that there would be no time commitment, so exactly what my service might entail was a little vague. But there would be a press release announcing my appointment to my local paper. And agreeing to serve would give me a chance to meet top Republicans like the Speaker of the House, "perhaps even President Bush," and give them my thoughts. So I'd have access to them on the issues that concerned my business.

They'd also appreciate it if I could contribute from $300 to $500.

"But if I can't come up with a contribution just now," I said, "I can still lend my name to the cause and be on the committee and meet President Bush, right?"

"No." No amplification, just a flat no.

"So my name won't help you without the money?"

"We need your name *and* the money."

"But without the money, you won't use my name."

"Are you a Democrat?" she asked suspiciously.

"Would the Republican Congressional Committee nominate a Democrat to serve on the Republican Presidential Committee?"

That's when she hung up. I'm not sure how that might affect my status on the committee. I expect I'll hear from President Bush himself in the next couple of days. We key business leaders shouldn't be wasting our time dealing with subordinates anyway.

In fairness I should mention that the Republicans have apparently scrapped these Republican Presidential Committee phone calls. Today, according to ABC News, they're calling "key business leaders" and telling them that they have been nominated for something called the "National Leadership Award." It's every bit as good a deal as the Presidential Committee, just $300 to $500.

Fortunately, very few salespeople and even fewer sales organizations ever sink to the level of politicians. I've known few salespeople in my life who would ever tell a direct lie to a prospect and fewer still who did it on a regular basis. The small con, based on lying and blatant misrepresentation, isn't a big problem in most sales organizations.

The Modified Limited Con

"Hi. I'm Barry, one of the boys in the neighborhood."

There are sales trainers out there who will hate me for saying this, but selling doesn't have to be difficult. Selling is the most natural thing in the world. Babies start selling the first time they realize their screaming can get someone else to do something they want: usually to feed or clean them, often at some ridiculous hour, long after room service is closed in the finest hotels, when nobody should have to be cleaned or fed. I've been selling for money since I was 6 years old, annoying the neighbors, hustling greeting cards door to door to "earn cash and win valuable prizes" as the ads on the backs of comic books proclaimed. I always took the cash.

My first real sales job—with an actual paycheck and W-2 forms and taxes taken out—came at 16, selling magazine subscriptions door-to-door. The crew chiefs would haul a bunch of us off to some distant neighborhood after school and on Saturdays and set us loose on the unsuspecting souls who lived there.

"Hi. I'm Barry, one of the boys in the neighborhood." That was the first line of my pitch. And I was Barry. No doubt about that. And I was certainly a boy, with all the raging hormones to prove it. And beyond question, I was in the neighborhood. But I certainly didn't live there. The memorized pitch implied—without ever quite coming out and saying so—that I was trying to build some kind of a magazine delivery route, carrying all the most popular magazines; much like a paper route, I suppose. No lies here, of course. The sales company I worked for sold subscriptions for virtually all the top magazines in the country. Every single customer got every single magazine they paid for— through the mail. Who ever heard of a magazine route anyway?

It's not the way to sell, and even at 16, I should have known better.

That's *the modified, limited con*. It's not blatant, and there are no actual lies, not literally anyway. And the customers usually get just about what they ordered at just about the price they agreed to pay. Often they get exactly what they ordered at exactly what they agreed to pay. Still, when those magazines arrive in the mail and they never see that "neighborhood" boy again, they're hardly good candidates for repeat business.

Making the Skeleton Dance

Of course most of us, as salespeople, never use any type of con, no matter how small, how limited, or how modified. But we're all too aware of the potential negatives, the imperfections, the skeletons that our products and services have. And many of us, perhaps most of us, are not as sold on those products and services as we believe we must appear to be to make the sale. Many of us do our best to steer our sales calls away from potential negatives or try to slip those negatives by our prospects unnoticed. We live in fear of objections, of the prospect saying, "Well, Jack, *Consumer Reports* says that your wheezle-whatzits are not only more expensive than the competitions' but they're also a lot less reliable."

The beauty of making the skeleton dance is that it can make dealing with a product's skeletons, a product's potential negatives, as easy as dealing with its strongest selling points. In fact, as I've said, it's a strategy that's designed to turn those potential negatives into selling points, even bragging points. Most skeletons— like price—are impossible to keep in the closet anyway. Others have an annoying way of popping out at the least opportune moment. Personally, I prefer to bring my skeletons out dancing, the way Helen Daniels did.

"Are our prices expensive? Absolutely. And why do we charge so much? Because we can." By the time Helen was finished making that particular skeleton dance, *more expensive* had become a positive—strong evidence that her company must deliver superior results. Why else would her clients be willing to pay those high prices? And *less expensive* had become at least slightly suspect. Would those other companies really charge less if they were good enough to charge more?

If you've got a potential negative the customer has a right to know about—or one that's bound to come out sooner or later whether the customer has a right to know about it or not—why not get it out there and get it out there loud and proud? Why not deal with it on your terms? Why leave it hidden away for the customer to discover later when you have no control over the situation?

And once you can make the skeleton dance, once you can turn those potential negatives into selling points, there's no longer a temptation to try to hide them or try to slide them by a customer unnoticed. There's no longer any reason *not* to sell with full disclosure. As we'll see in upcoming chapters, making the skeleton dance allows you to sell your product or service by detailing everything that's wrong with it and by explaining to the customer exactly what it won't do.

Truth: Bragging about a negative is much more fun than apologizing for it. It's also much more effective.

More Expensive, Less Reliable

But what happens when it's your product that *Consumer Reports* has rated as both more expensive and less reliable than the competition? Imagine pitching the general manager of a prospective account and having him suddenly wave that particular issue of *Consumer Reports* in your face, demanding, "So what have you got to say about this?"

"We saw that article too, Mr. Customer," you might say. "And we investigated their methodology. And do you know what we found?"

Mr. Customer can see where this is going, and he's already looking for a shovel, thinking it's going to start getting deep in there. He shakes his head, not in response but in disgust.

"What we found, Mr. Customer, was that *Consumer Reports* was *absolutely correct.*"

"What?"

"Our machines *are* more expensive. And it turns out they're also less reliable. In fact, of the seven companies surveyed, ours were the least reliable steam cleaners tested. *The very least reliable.* Now let me tell you why these are exactly the machines you need to turn your business around."

The skeleton is out of the closet and grinning. Now all you need to do is start the dance music. Your steamer cleaners are more expensive. They are less reliable. That's just simple truth. Why try to pretend it isn't? But you've run that simple truth through the Skeleton Protocol in a book called *No Lie—Truth Is the Ultimate Sales Tool*—you've learned how to make that skeleton dance—and you have only just begun to make your case. You've got the customer's complete attention, and your credibility has just gone from nonexistent to massive. And in sales, credibility is everything.

"So we're more expensive and less reliable," you repeat. "Why is that?"

"You're greedy?" the customer suggests.

You shrug. "We like to make as much money as we can. And we do that by selling the best machines at the best price."

"You just told me you're more expensive and less reliable."

"And believe me, I wouldn't lie about a thing like that."

"So which is it? Best machines at the best price or more expensive and less reliable?

"Both," you smile. "That's because our steam cleaners do the work of three different machines and do it better. According to the report in *Industry Standard* magazine, our machines get carpets more than 30 percent cleaner than standard carpet cleaners, drapes 45 percent cleaner than any other drapery cleaner, and upholstery almost 75 percent cleaner than any other upholstery cleaning system you can buy. We're more expensive all right. *Somewhat* more expensive than buying just one of those machines. Far cheaper than buying all three. And you know about our reputation for building a long-lasting machine."

"That's what people in the business say anyway."

"*Maintenance Digest* says that on average our machines last almost twice as long as any competitive machine. And they cost far less to use. And yes, because our cleaners do all those things, do them better and cheaper, and at the same time last longer, we are slightly less reliable. According to that article you read in *Consumer Reports*, that means a breakdown every 10,004 hours rather than their most reliable cleaner, which broke down every 10,982 hours."

"So that's 900 extra worry-free hours with your competition's machine."

"Almost 1000 actually. But what *Consumer Reports* never realized was that our maintenance contract guarantees our machines will be up and running again within 24 hours. And as you told me yourself a moment ago, you've never had one of our competitors' cleaners repaired in less than 3 days."

"Usually it's 4 or 5," he admits. "And sometimes I've got to ship the machines to them."

"And our service people come to you, of course."

"Always?"

"Always. And whenever necessary we provide loaner machines. So every 10,000 hours, one of our cleaners is down for 1 day—at the most. And every 11,000 hours, our most reliable competitor is down for 3 days—at the least. This is the kind of less reliable performance you can build your business around. That's why we're the brand that more professionals like you use to grow their businesses. That's why there are more than 3 million professional units in use today, and we're selling them as fast as the factory can produce them."

And this example isn't some special case. You'll find you can take this approach with the vast majority of the potential negatives you might find yourself facing.

Just One More
Interchangeable Beauty Queen

Truth: Candor creates credibility.

We all want to be credible. But too frequently we're afraid to be candid. That's why candor can also set you apart from the selling herd, that horde of salespeople your prospects spend so much of their time fending off.

What happens when most salespeople walk in a prospect's door? They're dressed like a salesperson, they look like a salesperson, they're carrying a salesperson's case and/or laptop. Everything about them screams *salesperson!* The prospect's defenses go up more quickly than an air bag in a head-on collision. Then the salesperson starts talking like every other salesperson; the prospect's suspicions are confirmed, and those defenses get just that much more rigid.

"Get the hell out of here. We don't want any," a dry cleaner once yelled at a sales trainee and me before we'd even gotten through the door.

"Of course you don't want any," I said, grabbing the arm of the trainee who was already backing out. "Who can blame you? But you need it. In fact, you have to have it. So get your checkbook out. It's not cheap." We hadn't even mentioned what we were selling yet.

"And you're on commission, right?"

"I'm not," I said. Then I pointed to my companion, "But he sure is. And the more you spend, the more he makes. And if you give us a second here, he's going tell you why you need to be spending more—and making him a nice piece of change. And why you're going to be delighted to do it."

Right away we were different from every other salesperson who had walked in there that day or that week, or ever. The dry cleaner obviously believed he had nothing to gain by listening to any of them. But if I'd turned on my heel and started to go, there's a good chance he wouldn't even have let us leave—at least not before he could find out why we were so confident, why we were so convinced he'd need our product that we could be so candid.

I once saw a movie on TV about the Miss Texas beauty pageant. I missed the first 15 minutes, but I'd watched for a half an hour before it dawned on me that the woman the film was following through the pageant might actually be two separate women. And the only reason that occurred to me then was that she seemed to be practicing two different talents: ventriloquism and Irish dancing. It was 15 more minutes before I was certain it was two different women. That's how close, how cookie cutter, at least to me, the women in that pageant were. A lot of people see salespeople the same way.

You walk in the door. You're wearing a suit, you're carrying a case, you smile ingratiatingly. Or you phone. There's that pause while the predictive dialer makes the connection. Bingo! You're a salesperson, not a human being, just a salesperson like all those other salespeople that your prospect sees, day after day after day. They're all pretending they only want to help. They're all paying lip service to customer service and consultative selling, but most are far more concerned with walking away with the biggest possible sale—and much less interested in the customer after the sale than they were before.

And this guy, this prospect, doesn't particularly trust salespeople. He might like some of them, but he doesn't entirely trust them. And he doesn't believe they have his best interests at heart. So anything you can do to separate yourself from that salesperson image is helpful.

There's nothing wrong with being a salesperson. There's nothing wrong with saying you're a salesperson. In fact, saying you're a salesperson rather than a *customer service advocate,* a *marketing consultant,* or a *small business adviser,* or any of the thousands of other euphemisms that companies come up with for their sales reps might be one way to differentiate yourself from the bulk of the salespeople that most businesspeople and consumers encounter.

"Don't forget, I'm a commission salesperson. The more you spend, the more I make. Now let me tell you why you need to be spending more and making me more." I've told prospects that thousands of times. And every single time it added to my credibility; it never detracted from it.

I was never ashamed to be a salesperson. I was never ashamed to be working on commission. What would I gain by acting like I was ashamed of either?

According to her business card, a friend of mine is a hospitality and heathcare consultant. She sells janitorial supplies. I recently went shopping for a mattress and was amateurishly high-pressured by a woman whose card labeled her a sleeping systems and solutions specialist. I hope she was good at the systems and solutions because she certainly wasn't much of a salesperson.

When prospects see a salesperson, they put up barriers, no matter what that person might call him- or herself. Act like every other salesperson out there and you're making it even harder to get those barriers lowered. And when it comes to lowering barriers and building trust, there's nothing like a little truth. Hell, it might even get you elected Miss Texas.

Besides, the first person you've got to sell—the most important person you've got to sell—is never going to stay sold unless the sale has been made with complete and total candor. The first and most important person you've got to sell is yourself.

2

You Are Your Most Important Customer

The silence stretched on and on. I had no idea what time it was when it began—when the broker asked her final closing question—but surreptitiously, I glanced down at my watch. I was relieved to note that it was still Thursday. The broker looked at her prospect, a stubby middle-aged man who owned a successful jewelry store. Her look had gone from expectant to blank and now to nervous. Her eyes shifted around the room and then back to the jeweler. I fought my natural tendency to take over the sales call. As a consultant here, I was only supposed to be an observer. The broker obviously had been through a certain amount of sales training. It was too much and not enough, but enough to get her into trouble and to keep us all sitting there waiting for hell to freeze over.

The sales cliché of course is that after the closing question is asked, *whoever speaks next loses*. That phrase says more clearly than anything else I can imagine how—in spite of mountains of BS to the contrary—far too many salespeople and sales trainers view the sales process. If they win, the prospect loses. One best-selling sales manual goes on for several pages, explaining how getting a customer to sign on the dotted line is in the customer's own best interest, almost a service to humanity. It explains how the salesperson is improving people's lives by bestowing her products upon them and helping poor unfortunate prospects who desperately want to buy and aren't up to making the decision on their own. All that comes just a few paragraphs before the author invokes *whoever speaks next loses* as the most vital axiom in selling. Two or three pages later, he compares selling to a bullfight with the salesperson the matador and the potential buyer the "grunting and stomping" bull. The close is the matador's "final thrust . . . ending the match cleanly." The bull is dead; the customer is sold.

In any case, *whoever speaks next loses* is true—at least partially true—when applied to mediocre salespeople. They're asking the prospect for a commitment, but they're afraid that after all their work, he's going to turn them down flat. The longer the silence continues after they ask their closing question, the more oppressive it becomes for them, and the more likely they are to start babbling, desperately moving the conversation away from the question they no longer want to hear the answer to—removing any pressure the prospect might have felt to supply an answer.

On this particular afternoon, however, our silent prospect, the jeweler, didn't seem to feel any pressure. In fact, he was the only one in the small cubicle who seemed comfortable. He sipped his coffee calmly. I had a sneaking suspicion that he knew at least as much about selling as the broker. She turned toward me and rolled her eyes, exasperated with a prospect who apparently didn't understand the rules of the game.

"Well, got to go," the jeweler said. He was out the door before she could recover, calling back at us, "Thanks for the coffee."

Later, the broker and I adjourned to a conference room to review the sales call. "So what's the problem?" she asked. "I gave a good solid presentation. Heck, it's practically word for word the same presentation our superstar across the hall gives, and he sells everyone who walks into his office. I did my fact finding, established need, proved value, and created urgency. I had all the answers to all his objections down pat. I got my pre-closing commitments. I did my trial closes and tried six different final closes. And you see what happened. You know, I read all the sales books—even yours—and I've taken any number of sales courses. I was number one in my training class when I started with the company. I know more closes than anyone in the office. I could teach this stuff. I've got the techniques. But I'm not selling."

"Why do you think that is?" I asked. It was a classic trainer, counselor, psychologist-type question. *Even my books?*, I wondered. What was that supposed to mean?

"I have absolutely no idea," she insisted vehemently. "If you ask me, I'm one of the best salespeople in the office. But I'm not selling anything to anybody."

"You know there's more passion in your voice right now than I've heard from you all morning. And of course passion sells. Conviction sells. Honesty sells."

"Yeah, I know." She smiled. "And once you can fake those, you can sell anything to anyone."

"Except yourself."

One of the Boys
in the Neighborhood Revisited

Way back when I was 16 and selling those magazine subscriptions, I learned a lesson that no one who wants to sell anything to anyone should ever forget. We kids would generate the leads, which we'd hand off to the crew chief who would go in and close the sale. I was the top kid in the office. I set more appointments that led to more sales than anybody else, and I was constantly being called up to role-play in front of the other "boys in the neighborhood." I thought I was as slick as Vaseline on a marble floor. Since we were paid on a bonus system and money was our true measurement of success, most of my peers agreed with me. And as far as I could see, I was getting better and better.

One day I was working with Terry, the number-one crew chief and the top closer in the company. I was pitching a middle-aged woman through her screen door, and Terry was standing just out of sight, listening. I was in peak form and 16 years old and showing off, and damn, I was good. The prospect was wary, coming up with a number of objections, but no matter which way she tried to squirm, I was there first waiting for her. I had her boxed in—wrapped up with a pink ribbon tied around her. She was all ready for Terry to move in for the close. I handed her off to him and went off to work my magic farther down the street.

Later, Terry came out of the call holding a contract. He caught up with me on the sidewalk in front of a house where I'd just finished another pitch. The first thing he said was, "You know something? You're the best salesman I've ever seen."

"Really?" I mean I knew I was good, but this was astonishing!

He nodded. "And that lead you just got, she said the same thing."

"No kidding. Well that's gre . . ."

"There's only one small problem." Terry held the unsigned contract up in front of my face and slowly—very slowly—tore it up in eight or nine pieces. Then he stuffed them into my shirt pocket. (The company might have been a bit shaky on some of the stricter elements of honesty, but they were way ahead of their time about littering. They knew it was very bad PR.) "The problem is that you aren't supposed to be a great salesman; you're supposed to be *one of the kids in the neighborhood.*"

Truth: When you're dealing with a good salesperson, you might think, "Boy, this guy is a great salesperson." When you really are with a great salesperson, you think you're with one of the kids in the neighborhood.

If you aren't speaking from conviction, if you don't really believe what you're saying, you're never going to be a great salesperson—not unless you're one of the best actors that ever lived. And if you're that good an actor, you'll probably be better off—and your customers will certainly be better off—if you just go to Hollywood.

Good salespeople are polished and professional and just a little slick. They've got a great pitch. They might be very likable, but they make most prospects just a bit wary.

A great salesperson might be as polished as the crown prince of Moravia if that's who he is, or he might be as folksie as Will Rogers or Abe Lincoln. He might be a disorganized sloppy mess and not particularly articulate, though he's always likable—very likable. And somehow he does always say just the right thing. Since he so obviously seems to believe in what he's saying, it doesn't seem to be a pitch. He "just seems to make a lot of sense." And he is never slick. He's genuine. The longer he talks, the less wary the prospect becomes. When the time comes for the great salesperson to close, buying from him is often as natural and as easy as ordering a fine meal at a favorite restaurant.

Great salespeople are aggressive and persistent and non-threatening, which means they're subtle and likable enough that few ever perceive them as aggressive and persistent.

If the prospect tells you you're a great salesperson, you aren't. What he's saying is that he feels that he's being "sold" something he would never purchase on his own. He may rollover and buy, but he won't be happy about it. He won't be happy to see you on your next visit, and he's far more likely to develop buyer's remorse and recontact you the next day.

To me, the highest praise a salesperson can receive from a prospect is simply, "You make a lot of sense." People who say that don't feel sold; they feel their needs are being met. Of course they may never have realized they had those needs until the rep walked through the door. And I guarantee they'll buy more from the salesperson who appears to make sense than from anyone they consider "a great salesperson."

Most great salespeople are great—they make a lot of sense—because they understand that the first, the most important, and the most difficult prospect they need to sell is themselves.

Getting Convicted

Like me, when I was "one of the boys in the neighborhood," are you trying to sell something to your customers that you're not entirely sold on yourself? As I said earlier, as salespeople, far too many of us are not as sold on our products and services as we believe we must appear to be in order to convince our prospects to buy. Far too often what we wish were true about our products and services—sometimes even what we say or at least imply about them—fails to match up with what we've discovered to be true. And if you're not sold on what you're selling, your sales presentations are never going to ring entirely true; you're never going to tap into the power that comes from genuine conviction.

But how do you become a true believer in a product that just might not be the best product of its kind in the marketplace? How do you sell that product to yourself when, better than anyone else, you know every scar, every imperfection, every negative about it?

You can't do it by ignoring those negatives. You can't do it by pretending they don't exist. You can't do it—at least not in the long term—by deluding or kidding yourself. But you can do it if you can honestly turn those negatives into positives, turn those drawbacks into selling points and even bragging points. You can do it if you can honestly make the skeleton dance for yourself.

Which brings us to the *Skeleton Protocol.*

Indroducing the Skeleton Protocol

The Skeleton Protocol is the easiest, most systematic way I know to make the skeleton dance, whatever that skeleton might be. It will help you reach a more thorough understanding of whatever you might be selling. It will help you sell those products and services first to yourself and then to your customers. It will flat out make you money—quite possibly a lot of money.

We'll be examining each step of the protocol in greater detail in subsequent chapters. But the seven basic steps are really quite simple and for the most part straightforward.

The Skeleton Protocol

1. Become your own most difficult prospect. Own up to the negative. Understand the potential downside to your customers as completely as possible.

2. List as many positives as you can about the negative: positives for your company, for yourself, and most important of all, for your potential customers.

3. Ask yourself why the negative exists. Is it *because* of a potential positive?

4. Ask yourself if in some way, in any way, the negative actually *is* a potential positive.

5. Ask yourself if the very existence of the negative is *evidence* of a positive.

6. Ask yourself if you can brag about the situation *on balance*, negative and all.

7. Ask yourself what, if anything, you yourself can add to the equation so you can brag about it with complete honesty.

3

Skeleton Protocol Step 1: Becoming Your Most Difficult Prospect

Know the Truth, and the Truth Shall Make You Rich—Maybe

"Now," the consultant said, "let's talk about what's wrong with your product."

"Excuse me?" the vice president of sales and marketing replied. "There's nothing wrong with our product."

"Personally, I hate your product."

"I'm sorry to hear that. Maybe we hired the wrong sales consultant."

The consultant nodded. "Maybe you'd be happier with a consultant who loves your product and doesn't see any of the flaws."

"Our products don't have flaws. Our quality control is unsurpassed."

"Everyone hates your product. From a sales standpoint, that strikes me as a flaw."

"We sell 70 million units a year! *Live and Love, Love and Live—with Safe-n-Sure.* That says it all, doesn't it?"

"You sell condoms. They're inconvenient, uncomfortable, difficult to use, and they kill the mood. The last one I used was so tight it nearly killed . . . Well, never mind that. They're a rotten product, and everyone knows it. How do you overcome that with a catchy slogan? Sure, you sell millions of units. But you don't sell a fraction of what you should be selling because, amazingly enough, even when the choice is between death and a little discomfort, a great many people are going to choose death every time. So I think that maybe your sales and marketing strategy could use some work. And maybe we need to start by figuring how to deal with some of those negatives."

Nasty, Painful, Evil, and Other Delights

Henry Miller said, "What seems nasty, painful, evil, can become a source of beauty, joy and strength, if faced with an open mind." I read Henry Miller intensively in high school: *Tropic of Cancer, Tropic of Capricorn, Nexus, Plexus,* and *Sexus.* Actually, I skimmed most of it. But I did read certain passages intensively. Very intensively, until my mother caught me. So I understand that Miller might not have been talking about selling strategy in that quote. But that doesn't mean it doesn't apply.

Obviously, you can't make a skeleton dance unless you're willing to acknowledge that the skeleton, the negative, exists. So step one of the Skeleton Protocol involves just that: lining all your skeletons up in a neat little row. What are the negatives that are giving you problems or that are likely to give you problems? Be as brutally honest as you can be. It may be something you yourself are concerned about, or it may be an objection others have raised or seem likely to raise. It could even be a customer objection you already have an effective answer for, but someplace inside you're just not comfortable with that answer. It may sell your prospects, but it's not quite selling you.

For each negative, consider the potential downside—to your prospects, to yourself, and to any others involved.

Some companies make this type of exercise an essential part of product development. At aerospace giant Boeing, for example, certain managers are charged with examining every new product's weaknesses as if they worked for the competition and figuring out ways to sell against those weaknesses. By the end of the process, they've usually torn apart their own product better than any potential customer or competitor ever could. And that's exactly what you want to do here.

If you can put your product or service back together again well enough to sell it to yourself, selling it to the rest of the world should be no problem at all.

4

Skeleton Protocol Step 2: Finding the Positives in Every Negative

It's easy to get distracted by negatives and focus on what's wrong to the exclusion of everything else. If you doubt this for a moment, think of the mass media stumbling over each other to uncover the dirt on every celebrity and every politician. Why do they do it? Because it works for them. Because we, the public, love it. It sells books, magazines, and TV shows. We take a perverse delight in discovering the skeleton in every closet, and the bigger and more expensive the house that closet is in, the more it delights us.

When there's an election, we vote for the lesser of two evils if we bother to vote at all. We weigh the negatives and vote for the lighter pile. A focus group was recently asked to participate in a mock election between three hypothetical candidates. The first candidate slept until noon, probably because he drank an entire quart of brandy every night. He began his career at one end of the political spectrum and then switched to the other end. He used to smoke opium. He presided over one of biggest military disasters in history. Twice, he was booted out of office.

The second candidate cheated on his wife. He listened to astrologers. He chain smoked, talked compulsively, and drank eight to ten martinis a day. On top of all that, he was suffering from a debilitating illness.

Candidate three was a decorated war hero and an astonishingly successful leader of singular determination. He had a sweeping worldview, ambitious goals, a plan for reaching those goals, and the determination to follow that plan. He never committed adultery. He didn't eat meat, didn't smoke, and seldom drank, never to excess.

These were the candidates the group was given to choose from. The first, the former opium smoker, was Winston Churchill. The second, the unfaithful husband, was Franklin Delano Roosevelt. And the third, the war hero, was a monster by the name of Hitler.

Truth: Negatives never tell the whole story.

Neither do positives of course. That's why salespeople who present only positives about their products and services are about as believable as the Pollyanna "let's all think happy thoughts" sales motivators who try to charge salespeople up with nothing more substantial than pixie dust. They tell reps how wonderful everything is without accounting for the real-world problems and sometimes less than wonderful reality those reps have to deal with.

It's a sad fact of our nature that we're more prone to believe 100 percent negative stories than 100 percent positive ones. But they're no more likely to be accurate.

There are of course negatives that can't be outweighed by positives. Charlie Manson would be difficult to elect no matter how many babies he kissed or how much he promised to cut taxes. I wouldn't want to have to try to sell Hitler to even the most gullible. (Though obviously, Goebbels and company did just that: selling him to a lot of people and for a long time. Not a selling job to be proud of.)

But the point is that the right positives can easily outweigh a surprisingly high stack of negatives. I don't care that Abraham Lincoln suffered from depression. A civil war that leaves 600,000 dead should be depressing. He was also an overindulgent father; he couldn't control his crazy wife; his high-pitched voice made him sound like a country bumpkin; and he kept telling jokes while the country was falling apart. Even in the North, many people thought that negatives like that made him a national embarrassment. I can wish nothing better for this country than that it might suffer many more such embarrassments.

The Benefits of Flimsy

Step 2 of the Skeleton Protocol involves listing as many positives as you can about the negative you're considering. We're not talking positives about the product or service but positives about the specific negative itself: positives for your various prospects, positives for yourself, for your company, and for anyone else who might be involved.

As salespeople, we do this all the time. Let's say, for example, that the negative is that the product is flimsy. Positives about that negative might be lightweight, easy to carry, more affordable, disposable. What ends up in your sales presentation might be: "It's not built to last and it's not priced that way either. So when something does go wrong, instead of having to invest in the kind of expensive repairs you'd have to make to protect your investment in a more costly product, you simply toss it out and get a brand-new one."

You know what's bad about the negative; what's good about it?

Dig into the Slag

List the obvious positives. "Fewer features? You're right, Ms. Customer, our stereos do have fewer features. Not only does that allow us to produce them at a lower cost, it lets us concentrate on getting those features we do offer right. Of course we could also offer nine or ten more features that no one really wants for just a bit more money. But then every one of our features would have to be produced far more cheaply. So we don't do that. Now let's talk about those features you actually want and need."

But don't stop at the obvious positives. Be as imaginative as possible. The other day I had a group of salespeople imagine that they were selling propane-powered strawberry harvesters that gave off a smell like a festering wound. Some of the more imaginative positives that they came up with included:

- Odor drives away fruit flies, mosquitoes, and other unwanted pests.

- Stench prevents children from approaching the machine and losing an arm or a leg.

- And, Mr. Customer, if your workers have been eating up your profits, snacking just became a thing of the past.

List every positive, no matter how small. *Slower delivery* might mean no UPS trucks double-parked and blocking the customer parking area. Don't worry if some of the positives you come up with seem minor or even silly. Smaller positives can lead you to larger, more important ones. Think of this as a brainstorming process, one that's a lot like mining. You may have to dig through a lot of slag to uncover a couple of gems, but those gems will make all the digging well worthwhile.

Every Cloud and Every Clod

A negative or a combination of negatives might be so serious that ultimately you'll never be able to sell your product or service to yourself. Don't let that concern you at this stage. For the moment you're just lining up the positives linked to that potential negative. And virtually every negative has them.

I remember the first time I made that statement in a Truth Is the Ultimate Sales Tool workshop. "Virtually every negative has its positives," I said. "Every cloud has a silver lining and all that."

"Like the Manson murders?" someone called out. I'd referred to Charlie Manson earlier, just as I did in this chapter.

Before I could respond some quick-study in the back of the room answered for me. "Exactly," she said with a bit of a laugh. "If every cloud has a silver lining, so does every clod. Charlie Manson focused much-needed attention on teenage runaways, on cults, on drugs, and on mind control. Those murders led to increased security in Beverly Hills and throughout Los Angeles and helped jump-start the private security industry. The fact that they also turned crime and trial reporting into a multibillion-dollar entertainment business might be a negative or a positive depending on your taste and the strength of your stomach."

What's Wrong with a Lifetime Guarantee? Plenty

Sometimes the easiest way to come up with positives associated with a particular negative is to imagine problems and disadvantages that might be caused by the alternative to that negative. Since your product or service doesn't have those particular problems and disadvantages, each one becomes a positive you can brag about. You sell E-Z Vac vacuum cleaners to retail outlets. E-Z Vac makes one model in one color while the competition makes 37 models, each of which comes in every color of the rainbow, not to mention a few colors never found in nature.

"Mr. Retailer, the beauty for you of dealing with a company that only makes one model in one color is:

- We have perfected that model; we're not trying to reinvent the wheel in 30 or 40 different ways. When we bring out a new model, it's because it's a genuine improvement.

- We can focus all our marketing dollars on promoting this one product.

- You, Mr. Retailer, don't have to tie up a fortune stocking all those different models. If you have one E-Z Vac, you have them all. And you have the best.

- Repairs are a snap. Your people need to be trained only on a single machine.

- You only have to stock parts for a single machine.

- Replacement parts are plentiful and inexpensive, and you aren't going to have trouble finding them in a couple of years because we don't make the model anymore, and it's not worth supporting the small number of each of the thousands of variations of different models and colors."

Note that you sell these points as your product's strengths rather than the competition's weaknesses.

Back when I was a corporate vice president, I was in the market for just the right customer relations management (CRM) program. Bill Jefferson was by far the most effective salesperson I was in discussions with, but I had serious qualms about his software. "Bill," I asked at one point, "isn't your program every bit as dated as your competition claims?"

"It sure is," he replied confidently. "It's been around forever. Nearly 4 years now. It doesn't have a lot of the competition's bells and whistles. It's *last generation* in a *next generation* world. Which is exactly why it's so stable: a well-tested, perfected, proven performer with thousands of satisfied customers and all the glitches and compatibility issues worked out. *Last generation* works. And it's a lot less expensive. *Next generation*? Time will tell. And up to this point, not many people seem to need those next generation frills. You just might want to think about letting someone else be the guinea pig for the next generation."

All the other reps sold their products as the latest and the most up-to-date (even when that might not be strictly accurate). Bill sold the advantages of not being either.

In another sales workshop, a rep told me he couldn't get car wash operators to consider his automatic scrubbing equipment because the competition offered a lifetime guarantee and he didn't. "How do you sell someone on the benefits of not having a lifetime guarantee?" he wondered. "How do you brag about that?"

"The easiest way might be to look at the problems and disadvantages associated with a lifetime guarantee," I said.

"What are the problems with getting a lifetime guarantee?" "Anyone?" I asked, throwing it out to the group.

Not surprisingly, the first hand that shot up came from an individual whose company offered a lifetime guarantee, though in an entirely different industry. He said, "Everyone we deal with understands that it costs more money to build a product to last a lifetime—or at least one that you can offer a lifetime guarantee on. Do those car wash owners really want to pay for a scrubber that will last a lifetime? That means that they're paying your competition extra to deprive them of the opportunity of taking advantage of whatever great new technology might become available to the industry. They're paying more so that in a few years they might be at a considerable technological disadvantage, perhaps costing them far more in labor and water and materials—and in damage to their customers' vehicles."

The car wash equipment rep nodded. "In 1982," he said, "I bought a Kaypro computer. It had no hard drive, just two floppy drives with a capacity of 191 kilobytes each. It cost me $1795 and had a 1-year parts and labor warranty. For $2900 I could have gotten a very similar computer with an amazing 10-year parts and labor warranty. Of course by 1986 both computers were completely outdated, and for just about the price of that guarantee, I bought a machine that was light-years ahead of either one of them. Why pay for equipment that will last a lifetime or for an expensive lifetime warranty unless you're reasonably sure that the equipment won't be outdated for a lifetime? And nowadays that's a difficult assurance to have."

Two years later, I happened to have a chance to ride with the car wash equipment rep. I watched him close a sale, and I couldn't help but smile when he came to the part of his presentation where he said, "Do you know what my favorite feature of our Kleen-Sweep scrubber is? My favorite feature is there's no lifetime warranty!" Then he told the same Kaypro story he'd related at the workshop.

Anecdotes and stories—reducing complicated issues to easy-to-evaluate mental shorthand—are of course great ways to make whatever point you're trying to make. And as you come up with your various positives, be alert for anecdotes and examples that can help you drive the point home.

Having a flimsy product with no lifetime guarantee and no choice of models can be just as advantageous as having a political candidate who takes mistresses, switches sides, and drinks like a Barbary pirate.

5

Skeleton Protocol Step 3: There's a Reason for the Negative

When Bad Things Happen for Good Reasons

There's a reason your product is less than perfect. Why does the negative exist? Often it's *because* of a potential positive. Positives that explain the negative are frequently the most effective from a sales standpoint. They can also be the easiest positives to uncover. For example: "We can't promise to meet that kind of deadline. In fact I can promise you we can't meet it. That's because we need to run enough tests to guarantee that your new custom-designed beams will meet every one of your safety requirements and pass any inspection." Without the negative (the delay), there is no positive (the certainty of passing the inspection).

Or, "Frankly, Janice, we are less convenient than the competition. Much less. And why is that? It's because we're so extraordinarily thorough. Instead of just filling out a questionnaire on a Web site, you're going to have our technical people crawling around your business for almost a week. It's hardly convenient, but that's precisely why we make so very few mistakes and why we almost never have a serious customer complaint."

When dealing with high prices, often the reason they're high is precisely because of a positive or several positives. There's a reason your line of swimwear costs more than the low-cost merchandise sold at discount stores, and it's probably a much better reason than the name of the designer or the logo. But even if the reason is "we just like to make more money" or "they pay me a lot for selling this line to you," ask yourself how the fact that the company makes more, or that you make more, is a benefit to your prospect. Possibilities include more money for better product development, improved market research, and more attentive customer service; more to lose if you don't deliver everything you promised; a huge inducement to make sure the customer is completely satisfied—that kind of thing. You can go on almost indefinitely about the benefits to the customer of you and your company being more successful and making more money.

"What you heard about the income I earn is absolutely right. I make an excellent living here. And I want to continue to make that living—or to make even more if possible. This means I have to make absolutely sure I'm worth it. And I need to ensure that —just like all my other customers—you know I'm worth it. Now let me tell you why you're never going to begrudge me a single penny of that money."

Or, "Would you really prefer to do business with a salesperson who's just scraping by? Who has to keep piling more and more products on more and more customers just to keep his head above water? Who doesn't have the incentive to watch out for your best interest or the time to do it if he wanted to? Who really has very little to lose if his customers aren't satisfied and start bad-mouthing him. That doesn't gel with the way you run your business, and I don't think it's the way you want to be treated."

And of course, ultimately, there's a reason you and your company are making so much money. A reason so many customers have chosen to do business with you. They all had the same choices your prospect does. They all had the same cheaper alternatives. But they all decided to deal with your company. That's why you're so successful. And it's not in spite of price. It's because of price. Price is what allows you to provide the quality of products and services your customers need.

Never be afraid of negatives that exist for legitimate business reasons. Nothing is more braggable. What you're saying is, "Of course we have this negative. That's what allows us to create this great positive for you."

Just make sure that the positive makes sense and is an obvious benefit to the particular prospect you're pitching. He or she is unlikely to put up with a negative to benefit someone else, as I've tried more than once to explain to my friends in the pharmaceutical industry. Saying "The drug is expensive because we have to recoup the cost of our investment" is a strong argument that many Americans buy—or would buy if they didn't see the same drug being sold at a fraction of the cost outside the country. Then the reasoning becomes, "We're charging you more so we can charge others less and still make money." And the argument that John

Smith should pay more for his prescription today so the pharmaceutical company will be able to fund the research necessary to create drugs that someone else might need in the future works much better with the population in general (who might need those drugs) than it works with John himself, who has to pay more for the medication he needs today.

6

Skeleton Protocol Step 4: The Negative's Other Edge

The Benefits of a Criminal Record

Ask yourself if the negative actually is a potential positive in one form or another. A potential negative is often a two-edged sword, and the positive edge can be an extremely powerful weapon.

"You seem like a nice guy, Jason. But why on earth would I buy anything from your company? For crying out loud, your CEO was convicted of consumer fraud."

"And conspiracy to defraud," Jason adds.

"And conspiracy, right. And let's face it, you're in an industry that's got a reputation for shady dealings."

"Probably a well-deserved reputation," Jason admits, "which is exactly why you should do business with us."

"Why I *should* do business with you?"

"Think about it. Right now our CEO is on parole. He claims he's reformed."

"Don't they all?"

Jason nods. "You might not believe him. I do. I think he's truly a changed man and that he's learned his lesson. But even if this so-called reform of his isn't really true, do you think he's going to allow anything to happen that might get his parole revoked and have him sent back to prison?"

"Well . . . you'd certainly hope he'd want to avoid that."

"He's also being closely scrutinized by the D.A., by the press, and by consumer groups. You said yourself that our industry doesn't have the best of reputations. But for obvious reasons nobody else you might do business with is getting the kind of scrutiny we're getting. We can't get away with the slightest irregularity."

"That's for sure. One more major screwup and you're probably out of business."

"Exactly. If you have a problem with one of our competitors, maybe they take care of it now and maybe they take care of it right. Or maybe they live up to—or live down to—our industry's reputation. Maybe they just say, 'Sorry, it's not really covered by our warranty. Read the fine print. If you have a problem, sue us.' If we try anything like that, you go to the press or the district attorney and our boss might end up in prison. At the very least, because of our history, your complaint is going to get significant media coverage. It's going to cost us more to have you as an unhappy customer than it would ever cost to make sure you're 100 percent satisfied. We can't afford to take a chance that you might not be delighted. Plus delighting you and a whole lot more like you is the only way we've got a chance of rebuilding our reputation."

The CEO's felony conviction and the scrutiny it puts upon him and the company can be shown to make them—the CEO and the company—more desirable, more reliable, and more trustworthy. Thus, the negative (the conviction) is actually a positive. Or at least it's integral to a positive (a more trustworthy vendor). You might not want to rely upon this argument by itself to swing the day. But as a key part of a complete presentation detailing the benefits and safeguards the company offers, it not only could work, it has worked.

It works, even in a case this extreme. Trust me. Or maybe you shouldn't trust me. After all, why should you? I've never been convicted of a felony.

There Are Limits

Let's call this next company Dot Bomb. (Here, as in other places in the book, names have been changed and situations disguised to protect . . . well, mostly to protect the guilty.) At Christmas a few years back, during the height of the dot com fantasy, Dot Bomb's "vertically integrated, off-the-shelf, B2C e-commerce enterprise solution systems"—which I guess means *order-taking software* because that's what they sold—decided to go into business for itself. Customers were charged random amounts for products that they may or may not have ordered.

"Are you talking newlyweds billed $1.37 for living room sets or $0.63 for TVs?" I asked when the VP sales explained it to me later.

"Sometimes, but more often it was like an Ohio farmer billed $26,937.07 for a lifetime subscription to a magazine on Salvadorian salmon spawning. Or a 75-year-old minister billed $487,898.35 for a 'life-size, inflatable, anatomically correct companion (female).' "

"That could present a problem."

"You think? The newspapers, the TV, and the radio stations that picked up the story all seem to agree with your keen assessment. The good news was that we were finally getting the kind of PR coverage we'd been fighting to get for the last couple of years. The bad news was that it was killing our business. The question was: What were we going to do about it?"

Fixing the technical problem was easy. Within 24 hours the software was performing as flawlessly as the company's ads and brochures promised. Within a week, because of what they'd learned, it was far superior. And safeguards were in place to make sure that the problem could never happen again. Everyone involved believed the software was reliable enough to bet anyone's business on, including their own, which of course was exactly what they were doing, if they could ever get anyone to try the improved version.

Fixing the problem their sales force faced was more difficult. The screwup had become infamous, at least within the small circle of companies that might be Dot Bomb's prospects. There wasn't any hiding this rhino even if they had wanted to. But nobody was taking their calls anyway: Their salespeople couldn't get through to decision makers who'd been anxious to talk to them just a few weeks earlier. And if they did get through, no one would let them even begin a pitch. What good did it do to have the best product on the market if no one would listen? And even if people did listen, they weren't likely to believe.

So we helped Dot Bomb put together a sales presentation that began by admitting the problem. It mentioned the pricing debacle and the devastating effect on Dot Bomb's business. It continued:

"We screwed up. We screwed up good. So good we can't even think of asking people to trust us again. Who cares that we've fixed the problem? So what? Why should anyone trust us? They shouldn't. So we aren't going to ask people to. What we are going to do is create a situation where anyone who does business with us will have everything to gain and nothing, nothing, nothing at all to lose. Because right now, that's the only way we can get anyone to take a chance on us. We'll make it worth your while—and then some—to check us out. So . . ."

In the sales presentation, the negative—the pricing problem and all that horrible press—suddenly became a positive. The general thrust was, "Yes, we've got this problem. We're not only admitting it when cornered; we're the ones who are bringing it up. And guess what? This problem is exactly why you should do business with us."

Dot Bomb knew that their prospects were terrified of a recurrence of the pricing debacle. The company was betting the business that it would never happen again. If it did, they were out of business anyway. So why not assume all the customer's risk in this area? Dot Bomb had nothing to lose. So instead of selling the software and charging a large, flat, up-front fee as they had before, they set up a much smaller monthly royalty arrangement, in effect leasing the software. There was no billing for the first 90 days. And if the pricing problem or any similar software-related problem appeared again even for a few hours—which they pointed out was the total length of time it had happened

the first time—the software immediately became the property
of the customer, all previous royalties would be returned, no
future royalties would be charged, and all subsequent updates
would be free. And of course the software would be fixed as soon
as possible. After 24 hours, the company would face massive
penalties for each hour it remained unfixed.

The risk Dot Bomb was assuming was minimal. It was in fact
a risk they had anyway. In the long term, licensing the software
was far more lucrative than selling it, especially since their salespeople would be able to license far more copies than they ever
would have sold, even if the Christmas pricing disaster hadn't
occurred. Once it had, of course, they would have been lucky to
sell anything.

All in all, that negative was one of the most positive things
that ever happened to the company. Or it least it would have
been if they weren't simultaneously wasting millions on the full
range of dot com stupidity: ego-building advertising on mass
media aimed at millions rather than their few thousand potential customers; flying around the world creating useless strategic
alliances, often nothing more than link exchanges on each other's
Web sites; remodeling old warehouses into office space for maximum techno-nerd coolness. (So what if the acoustics were so
bad no one could hear anyone else. No one was listening anyway.) And of course, there were those ridiculously inflated salaries
for too many executives who'd never held any one position anywhere long enough for anyone to figure out they were every bit
as clueless as they appeared.

Bragging about the negatives can only take you so far.

7

Skeleton Protocol Step 5: More Expensive, Less Reliable, and Proud of It

Ask yourself if the very existence of the negative is *evidence* of a positive. "To be honest, working with our lead engineer can be every bit as difficult as you've heard. And why are our clients willing to put up with that? Because he's as good as it gets." The negative (the difficulty of working with this guy) is actually evidence of the positive (that he must be exceptionally good). Often positives developed from this step of the Skeleton Protocol take the tack of "And why do you think we get away with [that negative]? It's because . . ."

Why do you think we can get away with higher prices or faulty quality control or service that hasn't been what it should be or the fact that we're so slow or disorganized or behind the times or whatever? It's seldom presented in terms that are that blatant, of course—unless I'm the one doing the presenting. But the model for this is that pricing explanation we looked at earlier: "Why do we charge so much? Because we can. Now let me tell you why we can."

A few years ago, a huge and extraordinarily unpopular telephone company descended into a level of incompetence that would have been considered abominable in the Soviet Union in 1933.

"Maybe I should send my entire executive team out on one of these wilderness survival leadership programs," the CEO supposedly mused at one point. "The downside is that it probably wouldn't help much. The upside is that they might not survive."

Still, neither he nor any of the rest of the corporate brass seemed to realize how thoroughly the company was hated. But their Yellow Pages division and the Yellow Pages reps on the street certainly did. They'd walk into a business and customers would start complaining the moment they spotted the phone books under the reps' arms: a litany of one incredible injustice or telco screwup after another. When the directory reps tried to be good corporate soldiers and defend the phone company, they got laughed out of the accounts—or worse. At least one rep had a gun pulled on him. Others were physically thrown out of the store or office.

And the Yellow Pages people had nothing to do with the phone service. They were simply selling advertising. Eventually, the vice president in charge of the directory division realized that they had to come up with a way to distance themselves from the phone company that everyone hated or run the risk of killing the Yellow Pages cash cow that the company was milking so hard.

Desperate situations require desperate measures. The VP and his people came up with a plan and then trained a sampling of average reps to test it in the field. A rep named Susan got her first chance to put it into practice in a sales call on a bright young entrepreneur named Chad, the head of a major towing company and her biggest customer in that market.

"I'm canceling all my Yellow Pages advertising," Chad told her bitterly.

"Why would you want to do that?" Susan asked.

"I've had it with you people. The phone company sucks."

"Tell me about it," Susan replied, wondering how she was going to eat if he dropped all those full-page ads. Every time an advertiser reduced or canceled what he or she had purchased the previous year, it was charged against the current sales rep's commissions. Customers weren't the only ones who sometimes thought the phone company sucked. Not quite matching his tone, she complained, "Those of us on the directory side have to deal with these characters every day."

"Let me tell you what they did now . . ." Chad began, launching into yet another horror story, a typical telco customer relations disaster, even allowing for what was probably considerable exaggeration.

"If you think that's bad," Susan griped, "listen to this." And she came up with an even worse phone company story, initiating an orgy of disgust as they took turns berating the parent organization of the division she worked for. The leadership of the directory division had all signed off on this strategy, but no one ever seemed to be completely sure whether or not anyone had actually cleared it with the telephone company's top brass. Still, the top brass didn't have to face their irate customers—customers who, as a matter of literal fact, happened to be right.

It's easy and fun to hate the phone company, especially one as inept as this one was, and in no time Chad and Susan were clearly on the same side, having a wonderful time trashing their common enemy. Then she deftly shifted the conversation to Chad's Yellow Pages advertising.

"Sorry, Susan, but every penny I spend with you makes these &^%!* richer. And I'm spending $2500 a month," he said.

"Actually, with the rate increase, next year it will be $2798."

"Another rate increase!? Every single year it goes up 10 to 20 percent. How can they possibly justify that kind of increase?"

"Well, if you ask them about it . . ." *Them, not us.* "They'll tell you that the population keeps increasing, which means more directories are distributed. Your ads are going into more homes, which is more expensive for them and generates more business for you. They'll tell you that like everyone else their costs are increasing. That's all true. But it's not the main reason."

"So what's the main reason? Why do they charge so damn much money for this stuff?"

"Because that's what the market will bear, Chad. That's what the market will bear. They charge what they charge because they know—as you and I both know—that no one like yourself can possibly do business without Yellow Pages advertising. Even at these rates, it's still the most effective and cost-effective advertising you can buy: for you or any other towing company. I mean, look at these numbers."

She segued seamlessly into a strong, conversational, interactive presentation, nailing her case down with solid facts and figures. Then she said, "So what *we've* got to do . . ." It was *we* now, but the *we* wasn't Susan and her company; it was Susan and

Chad. "What we've got to do is develop the best possible ad for you, one that will get you the greatest possible response for your buck."

Then she helped him do just that. The next year, Chad was happy enough with that response and with Susan and the Yellow Pages division that he didn't have a bad word—or at least not too many bad words—to say about the phone company. Not even when Susan subtly started selling him on the company and their genuine efforts to improve customer service. To be honest, it might have been another year or two before the *we* in Susan's presentation included the phone company. But it did happen.

This telco/Yellow Pages situation was an extreme case. And the directory people had tried everything else. Still, I almost never advise going third party: "It's you and I, Mr. Customer, versus them, the company I work for." Here they were selling the salesperson and the product to the customer, using the negatives to prove the positives. "I'm on your side but let's face it, it must be an amazingly effective product. How else could *they* get away with treating customers so shabbily?" And of course it would have been better if they had been able to find a way to sell the company, the salesperson, and product to the customer—negatives and all. To split the company from the product and the salesperson creates an unnatural schizophrenia that's extremely difficult to overcome.

Still, today this phone company not only gets more of Chad's advertising dollars, but even with the telecommunications competition they now face, they've rehabilitated themselves enough in his eyes that they handle all his local and long-distance service, his Web site, his interactive voice services, his paging, and his DSL lines.

8

Skeleton Protocol Step 6: Balancing Act

You probably think Benjamin Franklin was nothing more than a printer, an author, an inventor, a statesman, a publisher, a revolutionary, a scientist, a philosopher, and a famous lover. But he's also the father of a sales technique designed to push the undecided off their fences and muffle the splat when they hit the ground. (Though some historians claim the technique was first used a century earlier on Native Americans to close the sale of Manhattan Island in exchange for $24 worth of exceptionally high-quality trinkets and beads.)

According to the superstition and shamanism of selling, the exact wording of the Franklin close is vital. Since I'd hate to deprive you, I'll quote it verbatim.

The situation is this: In spite of the salesperson's best efforts, the customer just can't quite decided whether or not to sign up for that correspondence course. After all, it does cost more than her last car. On the other hand, her rendering of the "Can You Draw Me?" mouse on the matchbook cover was inspired—at least according to the school's expert evaluation—and her potential unlimited.

"Ms. Jones," the sales rep begins. He leans forward to gain her complete attention, gazing at her intently and sincerely, just the way he's been taught. "Ms. Jones, as you know, we Americans have always regarded Benjamin Franklin as one of our very wisest men."

He pulls out a sheet of paper and a pen. Ms. Jones wonders if he's going to ask her to draw Ben Franklin, which will probably be a lot more difficult than the mouse. But he continues.

"Whenever old Ben found himself with a decision such as you've got here today, he felt pretty much like you do. If it was the right thing, he wanted to do it. If it was the wrong thing, he wanted to avoid it. So what old Ben would do is pull out a piece of plain white paper and draw a line down the middle."

The rep draws the line down the middle of the sheet. "On the left side," he says, "Ben would write the word *Yes*. On the other side, he'd write the word *No*." He does the same. "Under the *Yes*, Ben would list all the reasons in favor of the thing. Under the *No*, he'd write all the reasons against it. When he was through, he'd count up the reasons in favor and the reasons against, and his decision was made. So let's do that now."

Then he proceeds to lead Ms. Jones through all the reasons for signing up. And guess what? He's got a lot of reasons. She's heard almost all of them before, during his presentation, but she's hearing them again, and he's writing them all down. When he finishes helping her with that, he says, "Now let's figure out the reasons not to enroll."

He hands her the pen. And looks at her. Without another word.

Of course, all she can come up with is four reasons. Maybe five. He gives her that sincere look again, and nods his head. "The answer's pretty clear, isn't it?"

The last time I heard a sales trainer teaching the Franklin close, he told his audience that he didn't use it often personally, but that he couldn't think of one time when he had used it that it didn't work. Not one. He added, "By the time you finish it, you have the order and you've positioned yourself with one of the great icons of America . . . It's part of the excitement that gets the adrenalin pumping in sales."

Okay, but didn't that same great icon have something to say about a fool and his money? Still, how could you not like Old Ben's system, a system under which a positive selling point like "would make this nice salesman a fat commission" is given the exact same weight as a negative like "end of all life as we know it." I bow to none in my admiration for Franklin, but he's been described as the only president who was never president. Maybe it's just as well.

Still, the next step in the Skeleton Protocol is a bit like the Franklin close. I call it the Stuart scale after Dick Stuart, a ballplayer with the Boston Red Sox and a few other teams back in the early 1960s. Following the Red Sox may be where I first learned about bragging about the negatives. Few teams in the history of sports have had the negatives that have afflicted the Red Sox over the years. While the Stuart scale represents one of the most common devices in sales, it's seldom used nearly as effectively as it can be.

The Stuart Scale

In the days before the designated hitter, Dick Stuart was possibly the worst fielding first baseman in the history of first base. He was known not so affectionately as Dr. Strangeglove.

One time the public address announcer read fans the warning, "Anyone who interferes with the ball in play will be ejected from the ballpark."

"I hope Stuart doesn't think that means him," his manager groaned.

When the team bus drove by a cement plant, someone told the driver to stop because Stuart wanted a new glove. Every line drive was a threat to his life. With ground balls, he could usually get out of their way, but not always. Red Sox fans didn't know whether to pray for his safety or for a merciful end to his—and their—suffering.

But Stuart had his positives. First and foremost he was a prodigious power hitter. He once hit a ball that reputedly traveled over 600 feet.

The Stuart scale comes from imagining how his agent would manage to get the Red Sox front office to inflict him on long-suffering fans for yet another year. Because although he had negatives that could never dance on their own, *on balance* Dick Stuart was a braggable commodity.

"Yes, my client is probably the worst fielder in the league," the agent might begin.

"In the history of the league," the general manager might say. "Probably."

"That kind of defense costs us games. And there's nothing good you can say about that."

"No there isn't. But he can hit a baseball farther than any man alive: 400, 500, even 600 feet. He holds the professional record for most home runs in a season, 66."

"In the minor leagues."

"In a shortened season. His swing is perfect for that short left field wall in Fenway Park, and he creates more drama striking out than anyone else on your team does hitting a home run. Between the Dr. Strangeglove nickname and the home run record and the tape-measure shots, he's become a legend. He got a standing ovation for catching a hot dog wrapper that drifted down from the upper deck. For all his errors, for all the criticism, he's still the most popular player on the team. He's even got his own radio show. The bottom line is that he puts people in the seats, and with an eighth place team, you're going to make a lot more money with Doctor Strangeglove than without him."

Like the Franklin close, the Stuart scale involves putting the positives on one side of the scale and the negative on the other. However, the significant point is the weight, the importance of the positives versus the negative, not the number of positives versus negatives. If you can't find a way to make a particular skeleton dance by itself, ask yourself if you can brag about the product or the service *on balance*, negative and all.

Even if there's nothing positive to say about being a world-class rotten first baseman, on balance the picture is extremely positive. Stuart always ended up coming back for another season. And every year he made more money than the year before.

No Apologies

The key to using the Stuart scale in a call is never to apologize. We've all seen salespeople grudgingly, apologetically admit to a product negative, usually when forced into it.

"Okay sure, unfortunately our boats don't have a lot of speed but they're good boats, believe me. They've got . . ." Then they bring up all the positives they can think of, hoping that on balance the positives will carry the day.

To make the Stuart scale work properly, there should be nothing grudging or apologetic about it. And you're not apologizing; you're bragging, not specifically about the negative, but about the whole package the negative is part of.

"Slow? Damn right our ships are slow. But they can haul more tonnage more economically than any other freighter in their price range. They're got an unbeatable safety record, an even better dependability record, they last forever, and . . ."

Not apologizing doesn't mean you can't stick in a point or two that mitigates the negative, any reason why it isn't really as big a negative as it might seem. But you're not ashamed of the negative. Hell, you're almost proud of it. So after working in the mitigation, you might want to sell against that very mitigation a bit and enhance your credibility.

"Of course the design of our ships does allow them to load and unload much faster than anything of comparable tonnage, which means that all told, you'll get in nearly as many passages per year as those faster freighters that cost so much more to build and operate. But no question, out in the open water our ships are slow. Once you get them sitting still at the dock, they're in and out of there like lightning, but when they're actually moving . . . sloooow." You're not apologizing for the negative, you're not mealy-mouthing it or trying to explain it away; you're freely admitting it and perfectly happy to do so. You either brought it up first or if the prospect raised the issue, he gets the feeling that it would have been just a question of time until you did bring it up. And that means that when you do offer mitigating factors—any reasons the apparent negative you're so freely admitting isn't really as bad as it might appear—then those factors are much more believable.

9

Skeleton Protocol Step 7: Becoming the Ultimate Benefit

"After what happened last time, Linda, I'm amazed you can even show your face around here, much less ask for more business. Nothing personal, you understand. But your company just didn't deliver."

"Tim, we both know that last time our execution just wasn't what it should be. Not that it was intentional . . ."

"I'm not saying it was intentional."

"Actually, intentional or not, it really doesn't matter, does it? We screwed up. Only the results matter. And let's face it, our people dropped the ball."

"So how can I know they won't do it again?"

"Actually, you can't. To be honest, Tim, with the merger and the kind of growth we're going through, until we can get all our new people properly trained, I can't promise somebody won't screw something up again. But here's what I can promise you. I'm going to oversee the entire project personally—every single step of the way. I mean every single step, hands-on, down to the smallest detail. And I don't think I have to remind you of how successful my track record is and why I can guarantee we're going to bring in a top-quality job, on time and below budget."

In step 7 of the Skeleton Protocol, ask yourself what you can bring to the situation so you can brag about it with complete honesty. *You* become the difference between a negative and a positive situation—between a deal you can't sell to yourself and your prospects and one that you can.

Obviously, one of the best ways to do this is through massive customer service, devoting time and effort to making certain that the experience of doing business with you and your company is everything you need to claim it is to make the sale— and more. I don't know about you, but I've purchased any number of products and services because I was convinced that the salespeople cared about my satisfaction and would be there if I needed them.

Or maybe you can become a resource for your customers, a font of knowledge they can rely on: product knowledge, industry knowledge, or even just business knowledge in general.

If a meeting planner calls to ask about hiring me as a speaker and we don't think I'm right for her particular function, we'll recommend a speaker who will be right. If we don't know of one, we'll find one. We'll spend whatever time is necessary to answer her questions about hiring and working with speakers. We'll let her know that she can call us at any time if she has additional questions and concerns. Down the road, when she needs a business or a sales speaker—or when someone asks her to recommend a business or a sales speaker—who do you think gets the call?

Part of what your customers are buying—often a big part— is you. If you make yourself the ultimate value-added feature, you can be the final benefit that lifts your product above the competition and makes the situation one you can brag about, negatives and all.

The Rasputin Account

A stockbroker was trying to land a well-to-do contractor as a client back in the early 1970s, when the market was dropping faster than Richard Nixon's approval ratings. She wasn't having much luck with him over the phone so one afternoon she stopped by his office. It wasn't going any better until, searching for something to build a little rapport, she noticed a newspaper clipping mounted on a plaque on one wall. Accompanying the story was a picture of a little girl in a ballet outfit.

"Is that your daughter?" she asked.

It was the last thing she got to say for the next 10 minutes. The proud parent went on and on about the kid and her dancing with apparently justifiable pride. His daughter had even been selected by George Balanchine to perform in *The Nutcracker* at Lincoln Center one year. That seemed to thrill the contractor even more than it must have thrilled the girl.

A few months later, the broker heard that a world-renowned Russian ballet troop was coming to town. She bought two tickets at $17.50 each—which back then, with the stock market busily tunneling its way to hell, was a lot of money. She sent the tickets to the contractor and his daughter along with a warm personal note.

"Whereupon," says the broker, "the guy turned into what I call the *Rasputin account:* Nothing I did could kill it." Nothing. No matter how badly her recommendations performed, the contractor kept coming back for more.

Any number of other financial consultants can tell the same type of story. This is why brokerages teach their people that their business is not about making clients money; it's about building relationships. That's just not what they tell their clients, most of whom seem to believe they're more interested in making money than new friends.

Truth: Once customers believe you care about them, they'll look for reasons to buy from you. When they look, they usually find.

A Simple Trick, a Possible Bore

There is of course a trick to getting a customer to believe you care about him or her. The trick to getting a customer to believe you care is to care. Someone once said that quoting yourself is the hallmark of the true bore. That may well be true, but at the risk of confirming what you might already suspect, here it comes anyway. As Barry Maher (me) frequently says, "Concentrate on the *what's in it for them* and the *what's in it for you* will usually take care of itself."

You can concentrate on what's in it for you and still sell. As noted, there are salespeople out there who view sales as war and the customer as an enemy that must be overcome. They con the customer about who they are and how much they care, even if they tell the complete truth about whatever it is they're selling. Whether or not they have a problem with how that makes them feel about their job and their lives is their business. Again, none of this is about ethics. But the longer the relationship with that customer goes on, the more likely it is that their true priorities are going to come out. And when that happens—no matter how well liked they might have been before—they're immediately going to drop back down to the level of just another sales huckster.

Truth: It's easier just to care than to pretend to care.

A Customer Only a Mother Could Love

Caring can be difficult. We've all had customers who were hard to love, to say the very least. With all the thousands and thousands of prospects and customers I've dealt with over the years as a salesperson, a sales trainer, and a sales consultant, one individual in particular stands head and shoulders above the rest.

This is an incident from my own Yellow Pages career years ago. The prospect was a chiropractor who had just taken some ludicrous personality course, and he insisted on vocally analyzing his patients, his staff, and me as if he knew what he was talking about. This guy didn't need a personality course; this guy needed a personality transplant.

When it was my turn, he analyzed virtually every word I said, my body language, my inflection, and my clothes. All were wanting. He questioned my integrity, my values, my motives, my sales ability, and even my smile. I didn't smile or laugh enough for him.

"If you want to sell, you need to smile more and laugh at my jokes," he instructed. Now normally, I try to have as much fun in a call as I can, figuring that if I can make it fun for myself and make it fun for the customer, not only am I half way to a sale but I'm going to have a much better time even if I don't sell a thing. As far as I'm concerned, in life, in business, and in sales, he or she who has the most fun wins.

But this guy wasn't fun. I'd watched him dissect his receptionist and two patients while he'd had me cooling my heels in the waiting room. I wasn't about to fake a grin or a chuckle just to sell him something, even though he was considering a large purchase and we were struggling to develop a new directory in a new market. This was a sale the directory company needed, and the chiropractor genuinely needed the advertising. Plus, if I was going to put up with this individual, I was determined that I was going to sell him. This was one time in my life when selling was a competition between me and the prospect. And I was determined to win. But I was going to do it on my terms.

"Bill," I said at one point, suddenly dispensing with the title Doctor, "you don't like me. You don't like anything about me."

"Hey, you're the one who's trying to sell your crap to me. I'm not trying to sell anything to you. I'm just telling you that if you want to succeed as a salesperson, there are some things you need to work on." At that moment, I was the leading rep in the world for the Fortune 100 company I worked for—and I had been for several years.

"I don't like you either, Billy," I said, deliberately adding a slight sneer in my voice. Do not try this technique at home.

"Maybe you should get the hell out of my office then."

"*Probably* I should get the hell out of your office. But whether you like me or I like you is not the issue. I can live with you not liking me. Unfortunately, you're probably not the first person or the last who won't like me."

"I can believe that."

"And I'm sure you can live without *my* adoration."

"Nothing could concern me less," he said, though the tension in his jaw said otherwise. This was probably the most obnoxious person I'd ever met. My guess was that he was also the person who most desperately needed to be liked.

"But the point for me, Bill, is that I want your business, and I will do whatever it takes to get your business and keep your business and to make sure you're satisfied. The point for you is that you absolutely have to have an ad in this directory—we both know that. And there's nobody else that can do a better job of helping you design just the right ad for your particular business in this particular market and this specific directory than me." Then I explained just why that was true.

There's a certain type of psychological bully who only respects those who stand up to him, so this dose of honesty not only cut through the BS, it turned the chiropractor around completely. He bought full-page ads in several directories. From then on he did everything he could to earn my admiration. I never really warmed up to him, and the fact that I didn't made him actually seem to want to win my approval more.

But although I genuinely like most people and I very seldom run into anyone that I don't like, I was never able to overcome my strong dislike for Dr. Bill. Never. And the more obsequious he became with me and the more he bullied others in my presence to show his power, the less I liked him.

I couldn't have cared less about him as an individual. But I was determined to do the best possible job for him as a customer. If anything, I was even more conscientious because I didn't like him. I didn't want to lower my opinion of myself or lower my professional standards by shortchanging him in any way. So if anything, he got better service because of my dislike. I probably spent more time with him because I hated being in his company.

The result was a very nice commission for me and a large, long-term customer for my company. And Bill probably had the most effective chiropractic ads in our directories, ads that he eventually ran in every single phone book in which he was advertising because they drew so much better than the poorly designed ads he'd been using.

Some customers are hard to love. But even if you really don't give a damn about the customer—even if you hate your customers or just this particular one—you can still perform as if you care. You can still be just as conscientious as you would be if their welfare were your prime concern. You might be even more conscientious.

If you care enough about the results, you'll deliver even if you don't happen to care for the individual. (Of course you might want to do a better job of hiding your feelings than I did.) That said, the more you like your customers, the more you enjoy being with them and solving their problems and satisfying their needs, the happier you're likely to be with your job.

Guilt Trip

Mary Kay Ash, founder of Mary Kay Cosmetics, said, "Being successful in business isn't a matter of taking advantage of people who need your products and services. On the contrary, it's a matter of giving them so much value, care and attention, they would feel guilty even thinking about doing business with somebody else."

Salespeople serve two masters: our customers and our employers. In a very real sense, both are writing our paychecks. Therefore, both deserve our allegiance. Sometimes that can put us in difficult situations that offer no easy solutions.

Once I was working with the CEO of large corporation. Let's call him Algernon S. Shricklemorton. (CEOs tend to have plain vanilla names like Roger Smith and Jack Welch, and I don't want to get sued by some CEO with the same name as one I might make up to protect this guy. I figure even *my* insurance coverage can handle whatever lawsuits might arise from the Algernon S. Shricklemortons of the world.) Al and I were trying to sell another CEO, let's call him John Smith (what the heck, a fictional name is a fictional name), on doing business with us.

After a marathon negotiation, we'd virtually closed the sale—with the exception of three relatively small sticking points—when we adjourned for the night in exhaustion. I say *relatively* small points because something in the neighborhood of $150,000 was still at stake.

The next morning we had a golf game scheduled. We all met in the locker room at Al's country club beforehand. As was typical for him, Al started bantering with John about the outcome. The testosterone flowed good-naturedly, and they discussed various bets—typical CEO-level bets. I could see this might be an expensive morning, which is one of the hazards of hanging around in this kind of company.

Then Al suggested, "John, let's make the match really interesting and do some business at the same time. We've got those three unsettled negotiating points. How about this? If you beat me this morning, I grant you all three points. If I win, you give them to me. Either way, we're done and we've got a deal. It'll make the game exciting, and if I win, it'll make my new golf clubs deductible as a business expense. And even if you win, I can get Barry here off the damn clock."

I thought he was kidding. I'd seen large golf bets from CEOs before, but this was $150,000 or more here. And it wasn't their money. It belonged to their respective organizations. But these two were running those organizations. My job was to help Al close the sale, and one way or the other this would close the sale, though even sales trainers who still taught the Franklin close wouldn't try this one. I guess I should have been happy that nobody asked me to bet.

"Sound like a fair deal to you, Barry?" Al asked me.

"Sounds like the dumbest thing I've ever heard," I said, trying to pretend I was joking and not quite pulling it off. When he'd hired me, Al had told me he was "the best damn negotiator since the snake got Eve to trade Paradise for a bite of apple." I was just coming to realize that Al did indeed have a reputation as a snake and that it might even have been justified. However, during the negotiations, it had also become clear that, as a negotiator, he was a lot closer to Eve than the serpent. I think he secretly realized that. Still, I was confident that, in spite of him, we could get almost all of that $150,000 through negotiation rather than golf.

"If Barry's advising me against it, John," Al said, "that must mean it's a good deal for you."

"It's not a deal, it's a bet, I said. Somebody once said, *CEOs make deals. Suckers make bets.* I think it was me. "Maybe when the game's over, we can pitch pennies for paychecks."

But Al and John were busy playing titans of industry, both envisioning the great story they'd have to tell if they won. The bet was on.

After three holes, John was up by a shot. Then on the fourth hole, both of them hooked their balls to the left behind some trees. I was driving one golf cart with Al sitting beside me, and we were well out in front of John when Al had me stop on the way to his ball, saying he'd walk from that point. As I was about to drive away, I saw him kick at the underbrush and then move on a few feet and do it again. Then he hurried off toward his own ball another 10 or 15 yards farther down.

When I got to my shot across the fairway, I saw John searching for his own ball right around where I'd dropped Al off. He never found it, though he was "certain it stopped right around here." He was surprised, but he didn't seem at all suspicious. He took a lost ball penalty and eventually ended up losing the hole and the match.

Later, when John went in for a massage, Al and I were alone. I asked him about the incident.

"That was about $75,000 per kick, I made right there," he gloated. "That's probably more than the top kickers in the NFL make. Of course, there was also a bit of creative accounting involved in counting my strokes. And I just may have adjusted our friend's lie a bit back there on hole number 12. Just being helpful. I know old John-Boy likes a challenge."

I have no idea why he felt he could tell me this or why he thought I'd think it was clever, which he obviously did. But it put me in an untenable position. I was working for this bozo. Or rather I was working for the stockholders who owned his corporation. I didn't feel I could either be a party to these tactics or reveal this story told to me in confidence and kill the deal, hurting Al, John, and both their companies.

"You know," Al said, while I was mulling it over, "we need a company boat for entertaining clients and keeping the senior management amused. I think John just bought me that boat."

"No," I said after a moment. "John's buying the drinks—because we all know you were just kidding about playing for those stakes. No serious businessperson would settle issues like that based on a golf game."

That's when Al laughed and told me he did this type of thing fairly frequently. He called it his win/sin negotiation strategy. He thought it was funny. He didn't even seem to mind when I insisted that he back off and retroactively make the stakes merely drinks. He even turned that into a joke, telling the whole story to one of his cohorts at the country club later that evening. To him, it was all just a game: the business, the golf, our initial negotiations, his win/sin strategy. It was all part and parcel of the same competition. All played by the same rules, which were, very simply, whatever he could get away with.

Since I was involved in selling the deal, I had no choice but to step in and make myself the difference in a rather different way by negating the bet and then negotiating a fair deal with John on the three points still under discussion. Incidentally, we did get most of that $150,000 for Al's company. Negotiating the best possible agreement for Al and his stockholders was my job, and I'm pretty good at my job. I just wasn't ready to sell a package to John that I couldn't first sell to myself. So I made the sale and never ever worked for Al again. Fortunately, he lost his job 18 months later. No one outside the company ever knew why, and all the press release said was that he was leaving "to pursue opportunities elsewhere."

If Algernon S. Shricklemorton had been his real name, I would have sent him a box of monogrammed golf balls for his retirement.

10

When the Truth Kills the Sale

Some Skeletons Won't Dance

I was conducting a corporate training session on a stifling hot August day in Houston, Texas. Shortly after the session had begun, I'd realized that I had the flu coming on—and coming on quickly. The air conditioning in the meeting room had coughed on just long enough to break down, and my fever blended with the swelter of the day. Fortunately, the air worked great in the room where we were having the lunch break. Unfortunately it was giving me chills and blowing out a chemical odor no one else seemed to notice that was strongly reminiscent of damp sheep. I'd already pushed aside the fatty pastrami and the greasy French fries, though I knew needed to find something I could hold down if I was going to make it through the day.

"So . . ." began the young sales executive to my right, by way of initiating a conversation. I'd warned everyone not to get too close to me. But he was a 275-pound former college football player, and he obviously wasn't worried about some microscopic germs, no matter how badly they seemed to be kicking my puny little butt.

"So?" I answered to show I was tracking. Maybe I could get down some of the pudding.

"So," he repeated, letting the word hang there until I began to wonder if I needed to respond again. I was about to tell him that the pudding wasn't bad when he finally continued. "So what do you do, when you've gone through the entire Skeleton Protocol and you still can't sell the product to yourself. When that big fat ugly negative is still there—unbraggable—sitting like a rank, festering pile of pig manure, creating an ungodly stench in the middle of your sales calls."

So much for the chocolate pudding. I pushed it aside and gathered my thoughts. "I'd wait a week and run through the protocol again," I said. I sipped my coffee and then gestured with the cup. "Sometimes the best ideas need to percolate through your subconscious for a bit. *Percolate through your subconscious,* I thought, *not a bad image.*

"You don't know my subconscious," he laughed. "It's more likely to percolate more pig manure. Or some kind of putrid sewer sludge like that coffee you're drinking."

So much for the coffee. I had a feeling he was right about his subconscious. "If you've done everything you can do with the protocol but you still can't honestly sell the product to yourself, then you do exactly what all good salespeople do when they find they can't sell something to somebody."

"You quit and move on down the road?"

"You negotiate."

"With yourself?"

I nodded, and the entire room began to spin. "You negotiate with yourself," I muttered, looking for something to hold onto. Then I said, and these were apparently my exact words, "But once the monkey rehabilitates the dreidel, there's no chance to recompensate your pumpkin. None at all. Remember that."

Remember that.

___

Negotiating with Yourself

Truth: As salespeople, we always want to have a better deal to sell. We'd always like our company's standard offers to be improved in ways we feel would make them more salable and put more money in our pockets.

Many of us do have some leeway to sweeten the deal, perhaps offering add-ons or rebates or discounts or concessions like faster delivery or additional training or free installation. As a general rule, the less effective the salesperson, the more he relies on these sweeteners and the sooner he offers them to the prospect. The better the salesperson, the more likely he is to sweeten only when necessary and only as part of the final negotiation that leads to the close.

Even the greatest salesperson sometimes needs to sweeten the offer to close a sale to a customer. The same can be true when you're selling your product or service to yourself. Sometimes—rarely—you can work through the entire Skeleton Protocol and yet you still can't honestly sell your product or service to your-self. If that's the case, you may need to sweeten the offer. If you yourself can't honestly buy the deal you're offering customers, you may need to offer them a better deal. You don't do this to make it easier to sell your product to the customer. You do it to make it possible to sell it to yourself.

However:

If your company's offer is fairly structured, if other sales-people are honestly selling it and customers are routinely find-ing value in it, you should never have to alter the offer in order to sell the product to yourself.

Never.

If other reps are selling it, and selling it honestly, if custom-ers who do buy it know the truth about it and consider it a fair value, then the problem is not with the offer. If the people who buy it consider it worthwhile, why don't you? Chances are your problem is not with the offer. Chances are your problem is with the fact that you can't sell the offer. Find out how successful salespeople are selling it and work on your skills.

Adding Sweetener

But let's say the Skeleton Protocol hasn't worked for you. And let's say that no matter what you might personally add to the package in terms of customer service or becoming a resource, you still can't honestly sell the product to yourself. You just don't believe that your company's electron micro-gizmo is as good a deal as you feel you have to claim it is to make the sale. However, the electron micro-gismo *with* the free extended training your boss lets you throw in is a deal you can believe in.

So you sweeten the deal. But when do you sweeten it? Do you offer the electron micro-gizmo *with* the free training as your initial offer? I wouldn't. I'd still work in the sweetener as part of the final negotiations that lead to the sale. We'll be talking more about that kind of negotiating in the final chapter, but the basic principle is first to sell the original offer and sell it as strongly as you honestly feel you can. Then when you do offer the sweetener, you sell that as well, so the prospect understands the full value of what he or she is getting. And you get something in exchange for that sweetener, ideally the commitment to buy. ("If you order today, you'll also receive . . ." is the most blatant form of the strategy, but even that works.) Whenever you give something in negotiations, you get something. After the sale, of course you deliver more than anyone expects.

A More Complete Offer

Depending on your company, there may be a lot you can do to improve the offer, or there may only be very little. You might be able to offer premiums, training, add-ons, express service, or additional payment options. Even if you can't do anything like that, there are often other things you can do.

Sanjay "Hap" Singhal sells voicemail and other messaging products to wireless companies, phone companies, and Internet service providers. Obviously, these are big-ticket items, and Hap has had as much as $75 million a year in sales. He's improved deals by such standard enhancements as speeding up delivery and installation; helping his customers market the product to their customers; and providing free services and price discounts in exchange for letters of recommendation. He's delayed his company's invoicing to match the customer's budget cycle and offered to make his product work exactly like the customer's existing software so retraining wouldn't be necessary. He's also signed up as the purchasing agent's doubles partner in tennis.

Kare Anderson, a strategic communication consultant, recommends partnering and cross-promoting with businesses in related fields as a way to improve the offer. If you're selling swimming pools, for example, you might partner with an outdoor furniture provider. You could bundle the pool with whatever pool furniture the customer needs, giving a discount for the package. Or you could throw in a free period of pool care that an aggressive pool service might be happy to provide to introduce their business to potential new customers.

Susan Gilbert is a speaker, an entrepreneur, and an award-winning author. Back in the mid-1980s, she was selling computer systems to banks and securities firms, which was not an easy sale. Computers were far more expensive in those days and did far less. Most of the decision makers she approached understood computer systems about as well as they understood Martian, and trusted them about as much as they trusted Mao Zedong or the KGB. Then too, there was only a tiny amount of useful off-the-shelf business software on the market, and most of that was intimidating, difficult to master, and not always customizable to the needs of a specific business. Every one of Susan's prospects had heard tales of corporations that had spent thousands and thousands of dollars on hardware that ended up rotting away in dusty basement storerooms. Susan's computers didn't seem like a particularly great deal to her prospects.

So Susan teamed up with a programmer who could create the specialized software to meet her various prospects' needs. She and the programmer made their sales calls together. She sold the hardware; he sold the software. They turned those computers into the type of outstanding investment Susan knew they could be.

What you can offer to sweeten the deal depends on your situation, on your company, on your products and services, and— perhaps above all—on your imagination.

Discounts

Truth: Offering discounts is usually the worst way to improve a deal.

Novice salespeople often try to increase their sales by selling at a discount. But if other salespeople are selling the product at full price to customers who aren't later feeling ripped off, the problem by definition isn't price. Customers are obviously willing to pay the full price—just not the novices' customers. Assuming that there is a need, the problem is that they aren't establishing value, first in their own mind and then in the minds of their prospects.

Truth: If you haven't established value, you can't sell a diamond for a dollar.

Of course, without the efforts of DeBeers and modern marketing, a dollar just might be what a diamond is actually worth. But after one of the most effective jobs of establishing value of all time, what diamonds actually sell for is another story altogether.

One summer while I was on vacation from college, I became a tin man, selling aluminum siding and roofing door-to-door in the Boston area. The business has a bad reputation, but our siding and our roofs were the finest available. Our prices were high but fair. In spite of what consumers always want to believe, you can't get the best without paying for it.

On the last afternoon I was with the company, I got the best sales lead I received that entire summer. Several weeks earlier, I'd sold a roof in West Roxbury to the Davenports. Now their neighbors, the O'Briens, had called in and asked for me. Their house was identical to the Davenports. They wanted the same roof— our premium roof, the most expensive product we had to sell— at the same price.

I had a plane to catch, but this kind of sure sale was as rare as free money. Last afternoon or not, I was a commission salesperson, this was a big sale, and as long as I wasn't dead and buried—death alone wouldn't have stopped me—I was hauling myself out to West Roxbury.

Naturally, we were having a monsoon at the time. I had trouble finding the house, parked too far away, and got soaked. I was cold and wet and I didn't have much time, but the O'Briens knew exactly what they wanted, and they knew the price. So I figured, why bother with a presentation? I just wrote up the order. Then as I finished filling out the contract, I realized that on that very day the company had started a new promotion designed to give us an additional closing tool.

This sale was already closed, but the O'Briens qualified for the offer. So I told them about it and said, "Because of what you're already spending, with this promotion you can have all new, top-quality gutters installed on your roof for just another $25." Even in those days, the cost of new gutters would have normally run them hundreds of dollars. And their current gutters were marginal at best. I flipped back to the first page of the contract and started to write it up.

Mr. O'Brien stopped me. "Let's just stay with what I told you I wanted," he said somewhat irritably. "I think we're spending quite enough here."

At first, I honestly didn't understand. To me, the gutters were worth hundreds of dollars. That's what I'd been selling them for all summer. To Mr. O'Brien, they weren't worth $25. The $25 was more money back then, but it still was only a tiny fraction of the normal cost of those gutters and a microscopic fraction of what the O'Briens were spending on the roof. The problem was that I hadn't sold him on gutters. I hadn't established that he needed them, and I hadn't established their value.

I felt terrible because in my haste I'd obviously short-changed him. I quickly tried to explain just what a great deal this was, but it was too late. He knew what he wanted, and among the things I hadn't bothered to sell him was myself. To him, I was simply trying to tack a $25 add-on onto my sale. He wouldn't even allow me to pitch it. I didn't have the time it would take to backtrack and try to sell him from scratch.

"Tell you what," I said munificently. "I'll throw in the gutters. My gift to you." *If you give something, you get something.* But I'd already gotten what I wanted. This was my way of working on the second part of that adage: *Then deliver more than anyone expects.* I'd take the $25 out of my commission.

"Okay," Mr. O'Brien said, completely unimpressed. He never even bothered to thank me. The fact that I'd given the gutters away only confirmed that low value he put on them.

With the condition of the O'Brien's current gutters and their budget, if I'd have gone out there before the promotion started and handled the call the way I normally did, in all likelihood Mr. O'Brien would have been delighted to pay top dollar to have our gutters installed. He would have seen it as a small price to pay for the amount of value he'd be receiving. As it was, he contracted for a very expensive roof without batting an eye but thought I was trying to slicker him when I simply assumed he'd want to spend another $25 for something he obviously saw no value in.

The Tijuana Shopkeeper

If you're ever in Tijuana, walk into a shop—any shop—pick something up, ask the price, and then try to leave. "Hey, where are you going?" the shopkeeper will cry. "You don't want it for $200? Okay, how about $125? No . . . Well, how about $95 . . . $70? $50? My final offer is $50 No? How about $30?"

If you have the option of offering price discounts, they should usually be a last resort. And when you do use them, use them in a way that might actually work. Too many salespeople offer discounts with about as much credibility as a Tijuana shopkeeper. Free discounts, like free anything, are worth what you pay for them. A discount will be far more meaningful to the customer if it costs him something. *If you give something, get some-*

thing—something of value, even if it's simply a testimonial letter or a recommendation to another potential client.

You can even try telling the truth. What you really want is for the client to close and close today. So for example, you might say something like, "What we've found over the years is that many of our customers don't end up buying from us until we've made two or three or even four visits. Not that they don't get the information they need the first time we're out there, but it's hard for people to make a decision. I can be terminally indecisive myself, so I can certainly understand that. But all these visits take up our time and keep us from seeing other potential customers. They cost the company money. So what we've decided is this. If we can close the deal on the first visit, today, and you can allow us to schedule the job at our convenience—within the next month but at whatever time suits our scheduling best—that saves us money, and we can give you the exact same job we discussed . . . for a full 20 percent less!"

Selling Your Product, Not Your Soul

If I hadn't grown incoherent with fever and started sputtering about monkeys and dreidels that afternoon in Houston, the young sales executive would have eventually gotten to at least one more obvious question. It's the question I always get at that point:

"So what do you do when the Skeleton Protocol doesn't work and there's nothing you can do to sweeten the offer sufficiently so you can sell it to yourself?"

"Then you have two alternatives," I say. "The first alternative is that you can perfect your acting skills and your sleight of hand, practice those slick responses that sound so good but you don't really believe, and brush up on the Franklin close—while Old Ben does 90 to 120 rpm in his grave, wishing they'd named the damned thing after old King George or Benedict Arnold."

"And the second alternative?"

"It's a lot simpler. You can just find a product to sell that you actually believe in."

As a consultant, a trainer, and a sales professional, I usually recommend the second alternative. But then again, I'm lazy. If I can't sell a product to myself, it's just far too much work to have to sell it to someone else. I'd rather devote the energy to selling a lot more of something I believe in.

11

Tell, *Sell*, the Whole Story, Phinneas

Our text for today's sermon is the following parable. The fact that it is a parable does not mean that it isn't true. Around Barry Maher & Associates, we have a name for a certain type of sales representative. We call the type, *Phinneas*, as in, "He's a %&*!# Phinneas." This is the story of Phinneas.

And it came to pass that I had an elderly VCR in my bedroom that liked to munch on the occasional tape. I'd never had a VCR repaired before. A friend of mine who's a bit of a VCR expert had even told me not to bother, it's better to put the money toward a new machine. Or even better, I could buy a DVD player, which were just coming onto the market, one with a remote control that could run every other electronic device in the house and probably program and target the occasional Patriot missile as well.

One look at that remote control and I decided that I should try to get the old machine fixed. Besides, I already had one VCR with more features than I ever used, on the TV in the living room. The very next day, I happened to pick up one of these freebie coupon publications at a gas station. Inside was a coupon—aging but still valid—from a place called Phinneas' Fast Phix-It: 10 percent off on the repair of any electronic equipment.

In addition to the coupon, Phinneas also had a full-page ad on the back cover. That ad was a thing of beauty—professionally done, with a great eye-catching illustration, and copy so strong it made me realize how lucky I was to have a broken VCR to take to him. An ad like that hadn't come cheap. I knew that, because after a moment I realized that—though we don't do a lot of work in the local area—this particular ad had been done for Phinneas by Barry Maher & Associates. Me & company. I didn't mention that to Phinneas on the phone because I wasn't sure I'd be doing business with him. Plus, he was rather abrupt. But I figured he was probably busy. He did seem to know exactly what the problem with the VCR was. And he seemed certain he could fix it—for only $45.

A couple of days later, I got around to taking the old machine in. But when I got to the address in the ad, one of the two signs in the window said "Computer Repair," and the other sign said "Closed for Vacation." I almost drove off, maybe to come back the next week, maybe to forget about it. But I wasn't entirely sure I had the right place, so I dropped into the auto parts store next door and discovered that Phinneas' Fast Phix-It had moved three doors down.

And there it was. I'd driven right by it, but the only sign on the place was the name on the door. Since the door was open, it couldn't be read from the street.

I hauled in my VCR, stepping into a confusion of VCRs, TVs, and assorted electrical junk in all stages of repair and disrepair. All the available counter space was full of old machines. Two men were hunched over TV innards. Neither bothered to look in my direction or acknowledge me or the fact that I was holding an old VCR, which was not all that heavy but not all that light, and that there was no obvious place to put it down. The younger of the two actually glanced up and made momentary eye contact before immediately looking back at what he was doing. I figured he wasn't Phinneas.

I stood there. After a few moments, which seemed a lot longer to me than it might have seemed to someone of my approximate height and weight who was not holding an old VCR—and in any event was very nearly long enough for me to decide to carry my VCR back to the car and forget about this place forever, and maybe tell a few friends to forget about it too—the elder of the two men finally looked up.

"Put it down there," he grunted, indicating a rickety leatherette barstool that left more VCR hanging over the edge than I was entirely comfortable with.

A few more moments passed. Eventually, the older man—Phinneas, I suppose—stopped what he was doing long enough to write up a ticket, even asking me my name and phone number. I also managed to get him to confirm that he'd call me if the job was going to cost more than $45. It wasn't until I was back in my car that I realized I had no idea when the VCR might be ready, whether it might be 2 hours, 2 days, or 2 years.

But what I really couldn't figure out was why on earth Phinneas was paying out all that money for advertising. And it turns out he was also in the daily paper and in the Yellow Pages under VCR repair, TV repair, and probably under several other headings as well to cover all the different gadgetry he fixed. Phinneas was forking over a minimum of $3000 per month for advertising.

He was spending $3000 a month for sales leads, which is what getting someone like me into his shop was, a sales lead. And if that VCR hadn't meant almost nothing to me—if it was any more than "let's see if he can fix it for about $50 or I'll just toss it"— me and my machine would have been out of there. Granted Phinneas might have known the type of customer I was, but that was the type of customer he was paying the *Coupon Clipper* to get.

Besides, Phinneas had no idea of what other potential customers I might know, with what manner of defective Phinneas-fixable electronic equipment, or what I might own myself. After all, at that moment I lived in a place that besides typically gorgeous Santa Barbara mountain and ocean views had seven (count them) computers, four printers, two VCRs, four television sets, five phones, two fax machines, two complete stereo systems, two elderly electric typewriters, assorted radios, God-knows-how-many tape recorders of various types, and I'm not even sure what all else.

Phinneas probably dreamed about customers like me—not that I was about to take any more of that stuff to him, unless perhaps it reached the point where I didn't care about it any more and it was either Phinneas's or the dump.

But guess what? It turns out that Phinneas got that VCR running like new. It took him almost 2 weeks—during which I never heard a word from him—but he did fix it. And for the $45, which is less than anybody else in town would have charged. So maybe I would have told people about Phinneas.

Maybe I would have. If he hadn't gone out of business.

The Moral of the Story

Obviously, Phinneas was not a salesperson. Phinneas could hardly have been less of a salesperson. Still, some salespeople—and certainly many nonsalespeople who want to sell—can be nearly as bad as old Phinneas when it comes to giving the prospect the type of complete information he or she needs to decide whether or not to do business with them. It's not just that they don't reveal the negatives and don't sell with full disclosure. They don't even reveal all the important positives. Thus, as I said, around here we call this type of a salesperson a *Phinneas*. It means he's much more of an order taker than a salesperson. And maybe he's not even that much of an order taker.

Boohkas?

Encyclopedia salespeople—when there were still lots of encyclopedia salespeople—had elaborate memorized presentations that could last up to 2 hours. But one day after CD-ROMs and the Internet had driven the print encyclopedia business to a particularly low point, a man in an ill-fitting suit knocked on my door, lugging the typical salesperson's case. He held up a volume of an encyclopedia that I had never heard of.

"Boohkas?" he asked, in a heavy if indeterminate accent.

"Books?" I tried.

"Boohkas," he agreed, nodding.

"I don't think so."

"Kids?"

"No, I don't think I'm in the market for any kids either. Thanks anyway though."

He nodded again, handed me his card, and then shuffled off to make the same offer to my neighbor. His card identified him as an education and training development specialist. It's hard to imagine that this poor guy had ever received any training of his own.

To be truly effective, making the skeleton dance—bragging about your negatives—must be part of a full presentation. And what's a full presentation? Simple. It's just all the information you really need the prospect to have before he or she makes the buying decision, the decision whether or not to go along with your recommendation. Like Phinneas, my friend with the *boohkas* was obviously an extreme example, but many, a great many, far far too many salespeople take so many shortcuts and cut so many corners in their presentations—they're such Phinneases—that much of their selling information never even reaches the prospect.

Tell—sell—the whole story. I know it's a lot easier to cut corners and take shortcuts in your presentation, if you even give much of a presentation at all. I also know that everything else being equal, you will sell far more if you don't cut those corners. And you'll eliminate a lot of those objections you hear.

Truth: If you're hearing the same objection over and over again, then in all likelihood there's something missing from your presentation—something that would answer that objection, or at least soften it, before it's asked. And that's a much more effective way to deal with an objection, before the prospect stakes out a position she might feel she should defend, before she's ever had a chance to question your credibility.

Let me repeat: If you're hearing the same objection over and over again, then in all likelihood there's something missing from your presentation—something that would answer that objection, or at least soften it, before it's asked. If you're hearing a lot of objections, your presentation is probably missing a lot.

Fact-Finding

Selling the whole story starts with the fact-finding. Trying to make a sale without the necessary information about your prospect is like driving off a bridge without checking for rocks in the water below. (Actually, there might not even be a river there; your prospect might not really be a prospect because, obviously, properly qualifying him is part of the fact-finding.)

Some reps are afraid to do a fact-finding, afraid of what objections, what potential negatives the prospect might bring up. But a good fact-finding doesn't make the sale more difficult by the issues it raises. It makes the sale far easier. It uncovers the prospect's hot buttons. It uncovers his wants and needs—even if they're wants and needs he might not realize he has at that point—wants and needs you can sharpen during your presentation. But most important, it uncovers those objections, those potential negatives, so you can tailor your presentation to deal with them in the most effective way.

Even beyond that, a good fact-finding demonstrates you're concerned with the prospect's needs rather than simply trying to shove the product of the month at him. It also helps create interest. We all know that the best way to come across as a fascinating conversationalist is to get the other person to talk about himself. Then too, if you ask about a problem he has, the implication is that you have a solution. Who isn't willing to listen to someone who might have a solution to his problem?

The questions you ask can also demonstrate your expertise and your understanding of the prospect's situation. A while back, we worked with a company that was having trouble selling Web site design services to small businesses. Almost all their prospects already had Web sites—usually terrible ones—but Web sites nonetheless. According to the company's salespeople, small businesses simply didn't understand the benefits of having a quality site. Of course the rep's managers were quick to point out that it wasn't their prospects' job to understand the benefits. It was the sales reps' job to make them understand. The question was: How?

The answer—at least much of it—turned out to be in the fact-finding. The company had assembled a great deal of information about a large variety of different types of businesses. Before each sales call, we had the rep check out the prospect's current Web site and come up with five or six or ten questions involving potential copy points that seemed to be missing from the information there.

The rep would walk into the business, for example, a glass dealer. The woman who owned the place would say something like, "Sorry, I have no interest at all in a new Web site."

"Of course, you don't," he'd reply. "Why should you? But give me 2 minutes. Let me ask you a couple of quick questions.

If just hearing those two questions doesn't help you with your current Web site *and* your other advertising as well, just say the word and I'm out of here, no hard feelings."

Nobody ever refused to listen to the questions. (Well, almost nobody.) The first question would always be, "Why should someone do business with you instead of your competition?"

Often that would get the rep nothing but a blank stare. This is the central marketing question for any business, and it's amazing how many small businesspeople have never even thought in these terms. But eventually, the prospect would come up with three to five answers. Astonishingly enough, those answers— the most important reasons for someone to do business with a company—would almost never be found on the business's Web site. Sometimes one would be missing, sometimes two or three. Often, very often, none of them would be there. Small businesspeople are even worse than salespeople when it comes to omitting major selling points and not telling, not selling, the whole story.

Then the rep would get into the remaining questions he'd prepared—no one ever stopped him after the second question— questions about other aspects of the business, other key selling points for glass shops that weren't mentioned on the site: if she dealt in noise-reducing windows perhaps, or shower enclosures, or sunroofs, or beveled glass, or storefronts, or skylights, or two-way mirrors.

Before he ever finished the fact-finding, he would have demonstrated—not just claimed but conclusively demonstrated, using the prospect's own words—that he and his company understood enough about this specific business to make a significant difference in its Web site. He'd be at least halfway to a sale, he'd have her complete attention, and he hadn't even begun to sell the whole story: explaining the detailed process for creating effective copy, running through the interactive demo, and wowing her with a huge variety of great sample sites.

Truth: Fact-finding is selling.

That said, you don't sell during the fact-finding, at least not ostensibly. You're not looking to contest whatever the prospect might say; rather, you're looking to gather information. You can toss in a sales point here and there, but selling usually interrupts the flow of information. There's plenty of time to sell later, once you've mapped out the opportunity and the obstacles.

So What Is the Whole Story?

Telling—selling—the whole story is not about regimentation or about management forcing salespeople to follow some script. It's about discovering what bases have to be touched to close the sale as easily and as honestly as possible. In a typical presentation, sometime before the sale is made, you sell three things:

1. Yourself

2. The product or service in general

3. The product or service from your company (as opposed to some competitive version of it)

Selling Yourself

When selling yourself, you sell your expertise. At least you do if it's at all applicable. Whether or not you have expertise, you also sell yourself with your manner, your appearance, and above all your confidence.

Your manner. Your manner should be well tuned to that of the person you're selling. You don't do this by mimicking them or by turning yourself into something you're not. You do it by bringing out that aspect of your personality that's most like this particular prospect.

Your appearance. This is an area where I part company with those who insist that a salesperson should always look as successful and professional as possible, no matter who his or her potential customers might be. As a salesperson and a sales consultant, I've sold to all types of businesspeople and to all types of consumers. To me, the salesperson who walks in to pitch the owner of an auto body shop in an expensive, dressed-for-success suit and tie is a guy who's just screamed out *salesman* at the top of his lungs. *Salesman* with all its most negative connotations: somebody slicker, somebody fundamentally different, fundamentally other than the guy who runs that shop; somebody difficult to relate to and even more difficult to trust. Why would you want to set up those additional barriers before you've even had a chance to open your month?

"People like to do business with people who are successful" is the mantra we're given to justify forcing salespeople to set themselves apart from their clientele. There's some truth to that. But people are far more likely to do business with successful people they can relate to.

My suggestion is to dress one level above those you're selling to. Be relatable—neat and professional, but relatable. Of course if you're selling to mechanics or plumbers, you may have to dress a bit more than one level better.

Relatability is crucial. It's easily lost, and once lost, it's almost impossible to regain. As I said earlier, I have no problem admitting to being a salesperson. I'll brag about being a salesperson. But I want to start out and remain as relatable as possible.

I once sold for a division manager who knew as much about selling as a nanny goat knows about needlepoint. He insisted on honoring the top salesperson in the division by hanging his or her picture in the lobby. I kept stealing mine and throwing it in the trash because whenever customers of mine came into the office after the sale and saw that picture, their estimation of me immediately changed. I was no longer a trustworthy, extremely knowledgeable salesperson who had made sense and helped them solve a problem. I was a supersalesperson who had *sold* them something.

I like to think that the reason I was the top salesperson was that I was trustworthy, extremely knowledgeable, and I made sense and made certain I was damned good at helping my customers solve problems. But once they saw *number-one salesperson* and the sales figures under my picture, in their own minds they became just another notch on the bedpost, another step on the road to my apparent goal of being number one and getting my picture on the wall. It was like waking up the morning after a great date and discovering that the person you'd been with was actually the number-one dater in the city, perhaps even a professional date.

I'm not slick. I don't want people to think I'm slick. I'm not putting on an act, and I don't want anyone to think I am. Once they do, forget about regaining their trust. The last thing I ever want to look like is a supersalesperson. Not unless being a super-salesperson offered some benefit to my potential customers: for example, if I were the top real estate salesperson in an area and I was trying to convince them to list their house with me.

Your confidence.   Nobody wants a doctor who says, "Well, maybe you've got a cold or maybe it's the plague or it could be just a muscle sprain. Take a couple of these white pills, they might do the trick. I certainly hope they do, anyway. Or maybe you should try some of the pink ones. If they don't work . . . Well, we've got a lot of pills."

Confidence sells.

Premature Articulation

Of course selling the whole story is about more than just delivering all the right information. Premature articulation will kill any sale. Are you providing enough information for your prospects to decide *not* to buy before you've ever given them enough to decide to buy?

Truth: If you can't control the sales call, you can't sell.

Today, my friend Paul Sheehan is a CFO of the Dyer Sheehan Group, one of the leading commercial real estate brokerages in

Southern California. But right after we graduated from college, Paul and I had a thriving business selling coupon books—full of discount coupons for meals, movies, pizza, etc.—to college students. Most of our salespeople were students as well. We'd front them the books, and they'd sell them wherever they could with no assigned territories—often selling mostly to their friends. Sometimes one of us would be banging on doors in the dorms or in student housing, we'd start to pitch someone, and that person would say, "Sorry, I've already made arrangements to buy one of those from . . .," and he or she would name one of our other salespeople.

At one point, our hardest working salesperson was the worst salesman who ever lived. His name was Mickey, and he had a gift for providing just enough information for people to decide they didn't want or need any of our coupon books. He was a friend and an exceptionally nice guy, and he burned a lot more territory than we should have allowed him to. It became almost impossible for our other salespeople to sell anyone Mickey had ever talked to—however briefly. The running joke became, "Sorry, I've made arrangement with Mickey not buy one of those from anyone."

Facts—both negative and positive—have to be revealed when the prospect is ready to hear them, not before. And this has to be done while respecting the prospect's agenda, which usually has nothing to do with listening to you give a full and complete presentation in the order you wish to give it.

Every salesperson on the planet has had it happen. "Mr. Hancock," she'll say, "you are going to be so astonished by what our new . . ."

"Never mind the astonishment. What's it going to cost me?"

"Cost? It's not a cost. It's an invest . . ."

"Just tell me the price."

"But price isn't . . ."

"The price! Now!"

"Well, it's $39.95, but when you consider . . ."

"Nothing to consider. It's too damn expensive. I can get the same damn thing for half price anywhere in town. Bye."

Of course he can't. And the rep could have easily convinced him of that. If she'd had the time. Price wouldn't have been a concern at all if she could have explained all the wonderful, life-altering, business-building features he would have been getting for a mere $39.95. But she needed to have delivered enough of that information—enough to have created a certain amount of immediate interest—before the issue of price could ever have been raised. Perhaps even before Mr. Hancock had any idea of what she was selling. If he'd had more interest, he might well have allowed her to defer the issue of price ("Don't worry. I'll be getting to that in just a moment, but first . . . "). At the very least, he might have been willing to listen for a while longer after hearing the price.

To give you the best possible chance of being able to present all your information—negative and positive—and present it in the most effective order, I always recommend using a structured presentation. The prospect of course couldn't be less concerned with your presentation plan. Often he'll take you out of it. He wants to discuss whatever points he wants to discuss, and he wants to discuss them now. And we all have various ways of dealing with those various issues that the customer raises along the way. But with a structured presentation, you don't allow these kinds of diversions to take you off track. You deal with them and then go right back into the presentation at just the spot you were interrupted. All your points get covered. The prospect learns everything he or she needs to know in the most effective order. You control the call. And the sale.

That's the theory anyway.

When the Customer Usurps Control

Of course there are prospects like Mr. Hancock who'll insist on running the show.

"What's the guarantee?" they'll demand.

"That's one of the best parts. Of course to understand our guarantee, you first need to know . . ."

"All I need to know is, what's the guarantee? I'm not interested in hearing your whole sales spiel. What is the guarantee?!"

Obviously, if a prospect insists on controlling the call, you can't fight him. When you fight a prospect, you lose. If he needs what you're selling, you both lose because you won't sell it and he won't get to buy it.

So you let him go where he insists upon going. If he won't allow you to get back into your presentation, you simply go about it another way. You work in your key points—the points you have to make—in the best way you can while you're dealing with his agenda. Often, very often, you'll be able to create enough interest this way to eventually slide in your entire presentation, though you might have to do it piece by piece. And of course your presentation should always be as interactive as possible—with this type of prospect or any other—never a monologue you're trying to force some poor soul to sit through.

So when Mr. Hancock says, "Nothing to consider. It's too damn expensive. I can get the same damn thing for half price anywhere in town. Bye," you say, "Half price? You can get a lot of our competitors' products for considerably less than *half* our price. In fact, that's why it's so astonishing that in the last 3 years over 1 million businesspeople just like you have chosen to do business with us. Do you ever have a problem with . . .?"

It's All Part of the Story

And remember, when you're in business, you are *always* telling—selling—your story. Once during a presentation to the sales force of a large office machines dealer, I happened to mention that I wasn't flying out until the next day. After I'd finished speaking, the local rep, whose name was Steve, came up and implored me to ride along with him that afternoon. He had an appointment at 2 P.M. sharp with a large printer, an appointment that had taken him months to get. Since I learn a lot more from making sales calls than I was likely to learn hanging around the hotel that afternoon, I was happy to go.

Traffic was much heavier than Steve expected. It was 2:03 as we pulled into the strip mall where the printing company was located. Fortunately, there was a single parking space right in front of their storefront. Unfortunately, another car, a Mercedes, coming from the opposite direction, was also headed for it. By rights it was probably our spot. We'd been there first, if only by a moment. But both cars turned into the space at virtually the same instant. Steve, however, was more determined or less worried about damaging the company car. At the last moment, with a sharp screech of brakes, the Mercedes yielded and we slid into the parking space.

With a rude gesture and an unflattering comment about our various ancestries, the other driver peeled off in anger, not for another open space farther down, but leadfooting it out of the strip mall altogether.

Steve flashed me a satisfied smile. "They teach us determination at Office Central. Now let's write up that sale." He grabbed his laptop, and we headed toward the shop.

The owner was standing just inside the front door. Compared to this guy, the man in the Mercedes had the serenity of Buddha. "That was a customer!" he screamed. "You steal parking spaces from my customers, drive them away from my business! You cost me money! That means, my friend, I have no money for your machines. None. I'd buy the worst piece of copying junk from the biggest crook in the country rather than pay a penny for the best machine you have to offer."

I couldn't wait to hear what kind of interest-creating remark Steve was going to come up with to overcome this particular buyer attitude. I'm sure it would have been great. Unfortunately, as he opened his mouth and cleared his throat to speak, the owner pulled out a baseball bat from behind the counter and waved it in our direction. The call was over.

Some sales organizations remind their premise reps that prospects frequently get their initial impression of them when they first drive up and get out of the car. One company that sells adjustable beds to elderly customers requires its salespeople to bring a cake to every appointment. They know that the little old ladies peek out the window the moment the car pulls up in front of their house. The rep is taught to get out, glance in the general direction of the house—without apparently noticing that he's being observed—smile broadly and pull out the cake.

I like to remind people that the sales process can extend far beyond the boundaries of the sales call. In April 2002, Dick Hamilton and his wife Audrey sold their home, drained their retirement accounts, and bought a linen supply business in a midsize town on the Oregon coast. To build sales, they called on every prospect in the area, spent enough on advertising to put them both through medical school, and cut their prices so severely that even the competition occasionally bought from them. Almost incidentally, they also put several thousand dollars into painting their delivery truck an eye-catching red, with their name, address, and phone number large and in gold on both doors and across the back. Which provided George Turley, the head of purchasing for the Hamiltons' largest prospective account—the account they had been pursuing since they arrived in town—with an unforgettable impression when Dick, stressed out and rushing from one sales call to the next, accelerated through a red light and nearly ran him down.

No sale.

Tell, sell, the whole story. And remember, everything you do up until the close can be a part of that story.

The Story Continues: Prophecy Fulfilled

Of course, what you do after the close is also a part of the story. Every time you deal with the customer, you're either fulfilling or contradicting the prophecies you made during your sales presentation. The next sale to that customer begins the moment you close the current sale—if not before.

12

Become an Expert
Witness

"Start building your team of sales sharks today!!!" That's how a
newsletter aimed at sales managers promotes itself. It's a "powerful stimulant for the minds of salespeople, powerful mental shark
food, if you will, for people who want to be as powerfully effective in sales persuasion as SHARKS would be!!!"

Wow. Or perhaps Wow!!! would be more appropriate. Funny,
I never thought that the *powerful* reputation sharks have was
based on their persuasive powers. I would have thought it was
based more on savagery, blood lust, destruction, and the rending
of flesh. And somehow I doubt if any company that subscribes
to this newsletter will start featuring in its advertising, "Call

Today and One of Our Powerfully Effective Team of Sales
Sharks Will Drop by at Your Earliest Convenience."

Far too many salespeople think of their prospects, even their
customers, as the opposition. They talk about "slamming them,"
"burying them," or "killing them." If you're a salesperson, that
kind of attitude leaves you with two choices in the call. You can
compete openly, in effect acknowledging that when you win the
customer loses. Or you can become a two-faced hypocrite.

The person you're trying to sell isn't the opposition any more
than you were the opposition when you were trying to sell yourself.
If there's an opposition, it's not the prospect but the Doubting
Thomas that lurks in the mind of every prospect—a Doubting
Thomas who's been right about salespeople and their claims all too
often in the past.

As salespeople, much of what we do is geared toward con-
vincing old D.T. of the error of his ways. The problem is that
Doubting Thomas isn't always wrong. And salespeople have used
their techniques on him before; they've gotten him to drop his
resistance, and he's been burned.

So how do you turn old Thomas around when he just happens
to be right? You become an expert witness.

The Word of God, Mixing Metaphors

As a well-known, self-appointed guru on sales, management, and
productivity, from time to time I've been hired to appear in court
as an expert witness. I love expert witnessing. You sit up on a
throne at the front of the courtroom and, like Moses down from
Mt. Sinai, you deliver the word of God to the mortals who sit at

your feet, hanging on your every word—even transcribing those words for posterity. And the attorney who hired you—like an attending angel—tosses you softball questions, which you proceed to knock out of the park. (A mixed metaphor, I know, but you get the idea.)

Conversations with Satan

Unfortunately, after your direct testimony comes the cross-examination. That's when the opposing attorney—otherwise known as Satan—does his damnedest to refute, or actually to get you to refute, weaken, mitigate, and/or contradict as much of what you just testified to as he possibly can. The first time you testify, your natural tendency is to contest every one of the points he's trying to make. After all, you are the expert, the authority. You've staked out your position, you've delivered the word of God, and this nonexpert—this *attorney*—is attacking it, by extension attacking you, and maybe even attacking God.

The cross-examination can quickly degenerate into argument, even a holy war. And that's exactly what the opposing attorney—Satan—wants because the more of a combatant he can make you appear, the less you look like the impartial bearer of objective truth. The more you look like a shark.

It's all right to be an advocate. Everybody already knows you're being very handsomely paid by the side that hired you. And in case there's someone on the jury from Mars who might not realize that, the opposing attorney will be sure to point it out the first chance he gets. And even the Martian is going to realize that they aren't paying you because you disagree with their position. Still, even as an advocate, the closer you come to wearing that mantel of objective truth, the more you grant the opposition their legitimate points, the more credible the rest of your testimony—all those points you need to make your case—will be.

You Are the Expert Witness

As a salesperson, you are the expert witness. You're confident, knowledgeable, and authoritative. You know what you're talking about. You've sold yourself so you believe what you're saying. Why shouldn't you? You're telling the truth. You make your case, your best possible case. You never have to deny you're an advocate or pretend not to be. Old Doubting Thomas wouldn't believe it anyway.

"I'm not a salesperson, Mr. D.T. I'm a lighting consultant."

"So how do you get paid, Mr. Consultant?"

"The company I work for, Komfort Kitchens, pays me, of course."

"For recommending the best possible fixtures for my needs."

"Absolutely."

"Even if some other company might have the best product."

"Well . . . I think you'll find that our products can meet any need you might have."

"So you're selling Komfort Kitchen products."

"I'm consulting on which Komfort products might be best for your needs."

"I see. And as a consultant you get paid by the hour or you're on salary—so you can be completely objective?"

"Well . . . Actually . . ."

The More You Spend, the More I Make

Personally, as I indicated before, I'm more likely to say, "Hey, D.T., I don't want you to forget—I work on commission here. The more you spend, the more I make. Now let me tell you why you need to be spending more and making me more money."

Truth is the ultimate sales tool.

Call yourself consultant or salesperson, call yourself Kip the Amazing Kitchen Counselor or whatever you like. You demonstrate your consultative approach by being consultative. You show your concern for the customer by *showing* your concern for the customer: in your behavior, in everything you say and do, not simply by claiming to be a consultant.

So you make your best possible case. Then you grant the other side, you grant old D.T., his legitimate points. When he's right, he's right. Why deny it? Sure you might be able to fool him for a while, perhaps even long enough to make the sale. But reality has a nasty way of rearing its ugly head. That's one of the worst features of reality. So Thomas is unlikely to stay fooled. And since being fooled is what he's always dreaded, when he finds out it's actually happened, you've lost him forever.

Besides, granting D.T. his legitimate points generates such massive credibility that your points—the points you need to make your case and the sale—should easily trump his. After all, that's what they did when you originally sold the product to yourself in the first place.

If you're confident in your product, your service, your offer, if you've already sold them to yourself, why should you be afraid to admit that the product, service, or offer might have a few negatives? To me, it's a lot easier to sell a product with a few negatives—particularly if they're negatives I can brag about—than it is to try to convince someone that I've got a perfect product, perhaps the only perfect product that's ever existed in the history of the planet.

Refreshing as Dirty Socks

A high-end janitorial supply company came out with a new commercial room deodorizer that had one obvious negative. "I hate to mention it," their customers kept saying, "but your new deodorizer smells like dirty socks."

The company-approved response, personally developed by the vice president of marketing, was: "Really, Marty?" delivered in an incredulous tone, followed by, "Most people find that smell refreshing. Like an ancient rain forest. Besides, the smell disappears after a few minutes."

Unfortunately, the room deodorizer smelled a lot more like dirty socks than any ancient rain forest—at least any ancient rain forest that didn't smell like dirty socks. And Marty was far more likely to believe his own nose than the rep's sales pitch. After talking with company chemists, a number of salespeople worked out their own, somewhat different response. A woman named Hazel was particularly effective.

"Dirty socks?" she'd say, "Hey, Marty, that's a big improvement. The original formula smelled like a piggery in July. And that smell is exactly what makes this the finest deodorizer on the market: it's the power of the deodorizer reacting with and destroying whatever rotten odors were in the room in the first place. Within 15 minutes, maximum, that destruction is complete, and the room is as odor free as twenty-first century science can make it."

"I have to admit, Hazel," the customer might say, "with all the business we've done, it was hard to believe you were trying to sell me a room deodorizer that stunk up the place."

"I would hope you'd find that hard to believe. But this deodorizer does stink—for darn close to 15 minutes. This isn't some sweet smelling cover-up. This is industrial strength odor removal. That dirty socks smell is the proof that it's working."

As I said, if you've been able to sell the product to yourself, your points should be able to overwhelm any negatives the prospect might raise. In this particular case, though, when the vice president of marketing found out about Hazel and the other reps' response to the problem, he took it as a personal insult. So the reps are still selling the new deodorizer as "refreshing as an ancient rain forest." At least they are when anyone from management is riding with them. And nowadays whenever bad news is announced—if quotas are being raised or territory slashed or commissions cut—Hazel or one of her hundreds of fellow sales reps is certain to shake her head and mutter in a stage whisper, "Refreshing as an ancient rain forest."

The Power of Positive Excrement

I was doing some training for a restaurant supply company and, on this particular day, was working with a new rep by the name of Rosemarie. She had an appointment with a restaurant owner named Herb, and we walked into his high-end dinner house carrying samples of the glassware she was hoping to sell. As we entered his office, Herb finished a phone call—what appeared to be a good-natured cussing out of his produce supplier—and focused immediately on the glass Rosemarie was holding.

He laughed. "Tacky fake-crystal crap like that is really not going to make it with our class of clientele. Now if you'll excuse me . . ."

Rosemarie stepped aside in surprise as he brushed past her. But she quickly regrouped and rushed to the defense of the company's product. "This glass is anything but tacky," she insisted defensively. "Your clientele would be delighted . . . "

I reached over, snatched the glass from her hand, and flung it toward the wastebasket in the corner. It clattered off the side of the basket and fell onto the floor.

"It's a piece of shit," I said, taking my language cue from Herb and stopping him in his tracks. "We happened to have that sample with us but that's not what we're here to show you. We want to show you glassware that's going to enhance the experience of dining at Herbert's, not detract from it."

I did a quick fact-finding and then launched into a presentation for the finest and most expensive glasses the company had to offer. Herb loved them—until he heard the price. Then they weren't really good enough. But somehow the glasses at a price two levels down from those "would be okay, I suppose," and we closed him on a good size order. When we were finished, I said, "You mentioned something about doing a breakfast business." He'd touched on it during the fact-finding. "So this isn't strictly a dinner house?"

"No, we're dinner only. I was talking about our other place, Angie's Diner."

"Rosemarie," I asked, "could you hand me that glass I tossed over there on the floor?"

She retrieved the glass, and I held it up to the light for Herb's inspection. It was unbroken. I banged it against his desk, hard. It sounded almost like glass but didn't break. "Like you said, Herb, this is anything but fine crystal. You could see that from halfway across the room. But it looks like glass and it feels like glass. It lasts like plastic, but it doesn't scratch. And wait until you hear the price."

Herb was right: The cheaper, long-lasting glasses weren't appropriate for his dinner crowd. But once he heard the price, he decided they were perfect for Angie's Diner. They were a good value for what they were. And they made a nice add-on sale toward Rosemarie's quota.

"I can't believe it," she said once we'd returned to the car. "First, you called the glass a piece of shit and then you sold it to him."

"How much did we sell in that call?" I asked.

"$1637," she said. "With more to come, figuring future break-age on the dinner glasses. More important, I got my foot in the door in two restaurants."

"And how much do you think we would have sold if we'd gotten into an argument with him about that inexpensive plastic glass?"

"Maybe nothing?"

"Maybe nothing. You would have been out a nice sale, and Herb wouldn't have his glasses. Besides, he was absolutely right. Those glasses are a great deal for the diner, but by his standards for the dinner house, they *are* crap. Why would I want to convince him that I'm nothing but a mindless hack—desperate for a sale—by arguing with him when we both know that he's right?"

Crooks and Bimbos

The point of that story is not that you should denigrate any of your company's product or services. Calling that glass "a piece of shit" was probably a mistake, made in the urgency of the moment and not a fair way to deal with a product of a corporation that had hired me to consult and to help train their people. If I haven't yet mentioned that I am not perfect either inside or outside sales calls, let me hereby state it for the record. I probably should have just tossed the glass toward the trash and said, "Forget about that thing. That's not what we're here to show you."

The point is that when the prospect is right about a negative he or she is raising, I never miss a chance to build my credibility by admitting it. The best idea of course is to raise the negative yourself before the prospect ever considers it. The second best idea is to admit old Doubting Thomas is right on target—whenever he *is* right on target.

And according to consultant Merrie Spaeth, former director of media relations at the White House, simply denying a negative can actually make the negative more memorable. Richard Nixon, questioned about his taxes, said, "I am not a crook." Enron CEO Steve Kean, discussing the company's creative bookkeeping, said, "It is not my intent to mislead." Jessica Hahn, the woman involved with televangelist Jim Bakker, said, "I am not a bimbo." But what stuck in everyone's minds? *Crook, mislead,* and *bimbo.*

All these people would have been better off if they had taken control of the situation and framed the terms of the discussion themselves. Rather than denying he was a crook, Nixon could have bragged about the negative and said, "You bet your life I took that large deduction on my taxes. I only wish it were bigger. Like every good American, I take every deduction I'm legally entitled to. And not a penny more. But I'll tell you what. If there's anyone out there who doesn't believe in taking all their legitimate tax deductions, I don't think that person should ever vote for me again. I'll struggle by with the votes of those who don't believe in overpaying their taxes."

Fortunately for the country, Nixon wasn't that good a salesperson. Nobody ever would have bought a used car from Richard Nixon.

Testing, Testing

One last note. What we're talking about here is granting the prospect's *legitimate* points: admitting he or she is right when he or she actually happens to be right. Frequently, however, prospective buyers will raise an issue to test you and see how you react to a concern they might have. If that concern isn't justified, you need to deal with it. The obvious way to do that of course is to explain the truth of the situation and support that truth with whatever evidence you have.

"I've heard there are safety concerns about this brand of tires," your prospect might say.

"Sure-Treads? On the contrary, not only have they got one of the best safety reputations in the industry, that reputation is backed up by test after test. Let me show you the numbers . . ."

Sometimes, however, when you feel the prospect is simply testing you to see how you react, it's more effective to just dismiss an issue like this, rather than giving it credibility by protesting too much. You dismiss it and then quickly segue to a selling point or even to a genuine negative.

"Of course in a really big storm," the prospect might try, "this type of large skylight will leak."

"Not in any storm that doesn't blow down the biggest part of the house. That's why this particular skylight is the industry standard for hurricane country. But there *is* a problem you need to know about."

"What's that?"

"The smell. The darn thing smells like dirty socks for the first 2 hours after the sealing coat is applied. After that of course the smell disappears completely, and you've got the finest skylight that money can buy."

"Dirty socks? Funny you should say that. That's what our motel room at the theme park smelled like the other night when we first checked in. The idiot at the desk tried to tell me it smelled like an ancient rain forest. I said, "Maybe an ancient rain forest full of dirty socks. But then, almost immediately, the odor disappeared, and disappeared completely."

"That's the way the skylight is. So what I do is buy all my clients dinner and two tickets to the movie of their choice for that evening. I guarantee the smell will be completely gone by the time you come home. In fact here's the movie schedule for next week. Which would you rather see, the new De Niro flick or . . .?"

13

Putting Those Negatives in Perspective

Beware of the Coconuts

We all remember the movie *Jaws*, and whenever there's a shark scare, sales managers at waterfront resorts all over the world find themselves drowning in questions from potential guests. And there are not just questions but cancellations, often large numbers of cancellations. Sales management newsletters notwithstanding, my understanding is that very few of these people are worried about the persuasive power of the sharks.

I'm a swimmer. And I speak at a lot of conferences and conventions. I spend far more time than most people paddling around in the waters off one resort or another. So the last feeding frenzy—the media feeding frenzy—on shark attacks made me paranoid enough to do some checking. As William Burroughs said, "Paranoia is simply having all the facts." Here are the facts, the reality of the situation, which I offer gratis to hotel salespeople everywhere. There's no need to thank me. Just send me a fruit plate the next time I'm booked into your resort.

Do people get killed by sharks? Of course they do. No one apparently has any idea how many billions of times swimmers went into the ocean last year, but of all those swimmers, sharks killed exactly 10 of them. *Ten.* Worldwide. Even if these sharks had somehow used their persuasive abilities to convince potential victims to go to the same beach on the same day and had gotten all 10 at once, if you happened to be swimming on that beach sometime that day—assuming an average beach on a hot summer day—there wouldn't be 1 chance in 100 that you'd be one of the chosen few. Even with *your* luck. But we're not talking one day on one beach. We're talking all the days of the year and all the beaches in the world: 10 people.

In New York City alone last year, 11,000 people were bitten by humans. Worldwide, 150 people a year are killed by coconuts falling out of trees. 150! Coconuts are 15 times as deadly as sharks. And bathtubs and showers are hundreds of times deadlier than coconuts. If you really want to live dangerously, don't go swimming, take a shower.

Forget *Jaws.* Remember Janet Leigh.

Perspective

Forty thousand dollars is a fortune. Or is it? It's a fortune for a second-hand Yugo. It's dirt cheap for a brand-new Rolls-Royce.

Perspective is everything. Great salespeople determine the perspective—the context, the scale—in which potential negatives are presented. When it comes to size—the size of an order, the amount of the price, the length of a contract—changing the scale can truly make the sale.

Truth: *It's not how big it is. It's how big it seems.*

Many salespeople hate mentioning any big numbers, like huge orders or high prices. But the big numbers are on our side. The bigger the better. It's the really big numbers that put the numbers you'll be trying to close on into perspective.

For example, I usually recommend throwing out a large price number sometime during your presentation, mentioning a particularly expensive order or product or the spending of a high- volume customer (without of course violating a confidence by mentioning the customer's name). Perhaps you can even work in all three. The idea is to turn the money the customer is spending—or that you're going to ask him to spend—into a much smaller number than it would have been when the call began.

You can also change the scale with your recommendation. Never be afraid to recommend the best, the largest, or the most simply because it carries the highest price tag. In all likelihood, it's got the highest price because it *is* the best. Why cheat your prospect out of the chance to buy the best? Then too the recommendation is the start of a negotiation process. The higher the negotiations start, and the more you can make the prospect want that bigger recommendation, the larger the purchase he finally settles on will be. Starting large makes that final purchase seem smaller and less expensive.

When I'm selling, I always do my best to make the prospect want the recommendation before I ever mention price. Even if she's thinking that it's going to be way too expensive for her, I make her want it. In fact, ideally, I want her wishing she could afford it but anticipating the worst.

I make my recommendation, and I shut up. Without ever having said a word about the cost. I wait for the prospect to ask. If she doesn't ask, I haven't made her want it enough.

So then she asks, "How much is it?"

My standard answer: "Ms. Customer, it's a lot. It's a whole lot. It's one huge pile of money." Then I pause while she's soaking up that image and imagining this incredibly high price, usually something much larger than the actual amount.

In most cases she asks again, "How much is it?"

Then and only then do I tell her the price. "Actually, it's $3417."

"And what am I paying for what I'm using right now?"

"$213."

"So that's . . .?"

I pull out the calculator. "It's $3204 more. $3417 altogether. It's a lot of money."

Not, *No, it's not really a lot of money. Not when you consider* . . .

I'm telling her it's a lot of money. But she's thinking, "Yes, he's telling the truth. It's a lot of money. But it really isn't all that bad." And it isn't. Not compared to what she was imagining just a moment before.

Now I know salespeople who would rather tear out their favorite organs than admit that their products or services cost a lot of money. "Oh, no," they'll insist." It's not a lot of money.

Not when you consider . . ." And then they'll offer two or three—or frequently far too many—reasons why a lot is really a little. Obviously, this tactic can work. Sales are closed this way every day. But put yourself in the prospect's position. (It shouldn't be difficult; we've all had this technique used on us.) The prospect's natural tendency is to throw up a barrier, a psychic resistance to such an obviously self-serving and counterintuitive sales pitch.

"Thirty-four hundred dollars might not be a lot of money to you," she's thinking. "At least not when it's coming out of my pocket."

On the other hand, I'm not only freely admitting it's a lot of money, I'm volunteering it. I might also tell her that it's easy for me to spend her money, which is usually exactly what she's feeling. I'm being straightforward—no tricks or verbal slight of hand to watch out for. I'm being credible. And because I made her want my recommendation and because she was envisioning a considerably higher price a moment before, that $3417 never seems like anywhere near as much as it would have if I were trying to push her the other way and talk her into believing that large was small.

And then—just when she's thinking, "You know it's not nearly as much as I thought it would be"—*then* I give her the reasons $3417 is not as expensive as it might sound.

"Yes, it's a lot of money," I say. "And it's worth every penny of it. And then some. And here's why . . ." At this point I might use exactly the same reasons the no-it-isn't-a-lot rep would use. But instead of resisting me, the prospect and I are both moving in the same direction. I'm not trying to talk her into anything; I'm being reasonable. And I'm obviously confident enough about the product to freely propose that she spend this kind of money. With the no-it-isn't-a-lot approach, the salesperson frequently appears to be searching to find excuses for the price, trying to explain it away or even apologize for it.

It's a small, subtle difference. Like the difference between night and day. And it can be the difference between a truly great salesperson—the one who "makes a lot of sense"—and the one who's perceived as a great salesperson because he sold the prospect something she later feels she never would have bought on her own.

"That *is* a lot of money," the customer might repeat to either type of salesperson after signing the contract.

"Not really," one type might begin again, "not when you consider . . ."

"It's a lot of money," the other would agree. "But if you think that's a lot of money, wait till you see what I sell you next time, after you see how well this works for you."

Truth is the ultimate sales tool.

Putting Your Positives in Perspective

Put your positives in perspective as well as potential negatives. When you make a claim, nothing enhances your credibility like hauling out a negative and using it to sell against your own claim just a bit.

"We have the highest customer satisfaction rating of any local home cleaning service. *The Daily News* just did a survey, and as you can see, our numbers are overwhelming. Now does that mean that we have complete customer satisfaction? Absolutely not. I had a customer the other day—an attorney—who was furious that we couldn't remove indelible red ink from his new couch. Sorry, but it couldn't be done. I didn't charge him for the upholstery cleaning, and we did get more out than I ever imagined, but unfortunately, nobody could have gotten that couch completely clean. That wasn't what he wanted to hear. So we don't satisfy everybody, but we certainly try. And as you can see from these numbers, it looks like we're doing a pretty good job."

Or "Daniel, now that I've told you all those wonderful things about our custom-mix asphalt surfaces, I also have to tell you they do take a while to set and dry. You're going have to close your parking area for at least 24 hours. This isn't one of those 6-hour jobs, and I know that can be an inconvenience. We need a full 24 hours, maybe 28 or 30 just to be safe. But for that temporary inconvenience, you get the best, longest lasting asphalt job on the market. You get to forget about your parking lot for years and years to come."

When using negatives to sell against your positive claims, the key points are the positives not the negatives. (This is not usually the part of the call when you want to deal with the issues surrounding those negatives.) To keep from being sidetracked, it's best to use negatives you've already dealt with or ones you've discovered the prospect can live with. If it's vital for Daniel to get his parking lot open as quickly as possible and you sell against your positives by tossing in "slow drying," you're going to be spending the next few minutes dealing with slow drying rather than whatever else you might have planned.

Changing the Scale for Yourself

If the most important person you'll ever sell is yourself, it stands to reason that the most important person you'll ever need to change the scale for is also you. If you're anything like me, from time to time, you may want to change the scale to put your goals and your efforts toward those goals in the most effective context, to help place your work and your life in the most meaningful perspective. The most meaningful perspective *for you*. Not for your boss or society or your friends or even your family. *For you.*

A while back, I bumped into a friend at a convention. A consultant, an author, and a speaker like myself, she'd had a dream for a number of years that she was finally beginning to act on. And she was running around excitedly, picking everyone's brain—so enthused she was almost throbbing. It was great to see. This was on a Saturday afternoon.

The following Friday, she woke up with bruises all over her body. Her husband was terrified, and he insisted that she go to the emergency room. She was more than a bit scared herself, so it wasn't hard to get her to go. Within 3 hours, she was diagnosed with leukemia. Six days and 137 units of blood later, she was dead—from complications of the treatment. She was 39 years old—and her dreams are still waiting.

But as sad and as tragic as that was, it's not the real kicker to the story. The real kicker, which should probably kick every single one of us in the butt every single day of our lives, is that there's probably no one reading this book who couldn't tell a similar story.

Yet how often do we find ourselves piddling away our days, focusing on the minutiae of the moment rather than the perspective of what we really want to do with our time, of what we really want to accomplish, of how we really want to live? Changing the scale for the customer can help you make the sale. Changing the scale for yourself can help you make your career—maybe even your life.

Creative Visualization

A little imagination can do wonders for changing the scale and putting things into perspective. Here are four simple visualizations I've found particularly effective for me in providing insight into the things I actually value as opposed to the things I sometimes think I value or the things I often act as if I value.

Visualization 1. This one should seem familiar. I'd be amazed if you haven't imagined it on your own. You might want to try it a bit more seriously this time.

You just won the lottery, and the jackpot was $137 million. After taxes and a small finder's fee to me for leading you into this fantasy, the lump sum payment to you is $73 million. What are the top five things you want to do with the money?

Visualization 2. The chairman of a major television network just called and asked me to give you the following message. Because of that thorn you pulled out of his paw at the MGM Grand Hotel in Las Vegas last week, he's going to give you an ad campaign on all the network's top-rated shows for any *noncommercial* message you might choose. What's your message going to be?

Visualization 3. Your fairy godmother's come down with senile dementia. She's got one wish left to grant, and it's all yours. But in her confusion, she's decided that it can't be something for yourself or your immediate family—and no, it can't be more wishes. What's your wish?

Visualization 4.   Here's an old motivational test I always like. Imagine a 6-inch-wide, 40-foot-long board lying on the ground. What would it take to get you to walk from one end of that board to the other? Certainly, you'd do it for $1 million or to save the life of a loved one, but what's the minimum you would do it for?

Now raise the board. Make it 5 feet high, stretching between two banks of a stream. It's 40-feet long so it sags a bit in the middle. What would it take to get you to cross it? Make the banks 10 feet high. Now what would it take?

Add alligators to the stream.

Now, raise the board to the height of a house and try it. Keep raising the board until finally it stretches from an open window on the top floor of one towering skyscraper to an open window in another skyscraper, 40 feet away. What would you cross that board to gain or to preserve or to protect?

How do your board-crossing priorities match up with the way you prioritize your time? Are you spending great hunks of your time pursuing things you wouldn't walk a particularly high board for? How are you using your career, the working hours of your life, your sales skills, and the trust you're developing with your clients to help you pursue the things that are really important to you?

14

Sex, Rejection, and Several Assorted Butts

A few years back, *Selling Power* magazine did an article on me. The opening caption read, "To his powerful and famous clients, Barry Maher is simply the best sales trainer in the business." Well, since *Selling Power* is one of the leading sales publications in the country—maybe in the world—I thought that quote was pretty great. I still use it every chance I get. I work it into casual conversations, slipping it in cleverly and unobtrusively. Someone will say, "Nice weather we're having" or "Think the rain will hurt the rhubarb?" and I'll say, "Speaking of weather, I was wondering whether or not you'd heard that *Selling Power* magazine said, 'To his powerful and famous clients, Barry Maher is simply the best sales trainer in the business.'" You need to be subtle about it.

Well, now that I've worked the quote in here a couple of times, let me say that shortly after that article first came out, I decided— great and eminent figure that I was—that I should give something back to the community. And directly across the street from me was a community college that just happened to be looking for someone to teach a class in basic selling to their 18- and 19-year-old business students. I'd cleared my speaking and consulting schedule to work on a book, so I was going to be home and available for the entire quarter. The salary was less than a pittance—maybe half a pittance—but I didn't care about that. I was giving something back.

I submitted an application along with some basic support material. I took the time to walk across the street to interview with the head of the business department. I never mentioned the *Selling Power* article or a few other credentials that seemed like overkill, but the hiring committee certainly knew that I'd worked with many of the largest and most successful companies in the world and that I'd spoken to and trained groups of all types and sizes.

They hired somebody else! They turned me down. Me! They rejected me—in favor of somebody who'd probably never sold a single thing in his life and taught the course from an astonishingly incompetent textbook on sales written by someone who didn't know a whole lot more than he did. Rejection!

Rejection

The first lesson I would have tried to teach that class would have been about rejection. Because we all get rejected. At a recent sales workshop—one I *was* hired to do—I asked the attendees what they would like to get out of the session.

"I hate hearing *no*," one woman said. "I'm sure most of us do. The best thing you could do for us would be to tell us how we can hear fewer *nos*."

"Nothing could be easier," I said. "Just make fewer calls. And in those calls you do make, the first time the prospect says no, just thank him and leave."

Then I walked over and—with a certain dramatic flare, I thought—scrawled on the whiteboard, 'Whoever Hears the Most *Nos* Gets the Biggest Paycheck.'

"What?" the woman asked in confusion.

"Think about it a minute," I said.

"No, I mean what is that supposed to *say*? I can't read your writing."

So much for drama. "Sorry. It says, 'Whoever Hears the Most *Nos* Gets the Biggest Paycheck.' The leading salesperson in the company is always the one who hears the most *nos*. The more *nos* you can hear in each call—without irritating the prospect—and the more of those calls you make, the more successful you're going to be. So you've got to be hardworking. You've got to be persistent. You've got to be good. Because the more rapport you build, the more interest you generate, the longer the prospect will be willing to listen, and the more *nos* you get to hear."

"So you've also got to be aggressive," she said.

"You've got to be aggressive without appearing aggressive. That means not riding roughshod over the prospect's concerns and not pounding the prospect with the exact same points over and over and over again. That's an argument, not a sales call. It means building rapport and creating excitement—or at least interest—and above all gaining trust. It may mean making your points in a number of different ways. It always means listening carefully to the prospect and dealing with his issues. It always means granting him his legitimate points."

It's Just Part of the Game

I recently moved from Santa Barbara to Helendale, California. Digging through the clutter of my own past, trying to decide what to pack and what to dump, I felt like an archeologist. One of the artifacts I unearthed came from my days as a sales manager. It was my copy of an evaluation I did after a ride-along with one of the best reps who ever worked for me. I wrote that on average that day, she'd gotten eight *nos* in each call before getting the final yes. Granted we were working a particularly tough market. But if she did her job right that day—and I'm I sure she did—not a single one of those prospects felt coerced or sold. If she did her job right, each simply felt that she'd answered their concerns and that she'd made sense.

Truth: Looked at from the right perspective, every no, every rejection, every failure is a small victory, a step on the path to ultimate success.

Motivating yourself to take those steps, and to make each step as meaningful as possible, is an essential part of your job as a salesperson, part of what you were hired to do, and part of what's going to earn you the kind of commissions you're capable of earning.

What would you think of a basketball player who was asked to take the game winning shot and missed—on 26 different occasions? Twenty-six different times! Still, this particular individual was resilient enough that he managed a make a decent career for himself in spite of those failures. His name is Jordan, Michael Jordan. He says, "I've missed more than 9000 shots in my career . . . lost over 300 games. I have failed over and over again in my life. And that's why I succeed."

Start collecting your *nos* as soon as possible. Rejection is only a big deal when you're talking about organ transplants.

Selling Is Like Sex

Another way to deal with the rejection and the pressure that comes with the average sales job is simply to remember that selling is like sex.

In sales we all know the importance of an interest-creating remark. And believe me, that's a pretty good interest-creating remark. It also happens to be true. When I'm speaking around the country and I tell audiences, "Selling is like sex," it doesn't matter how late in the day it is or how much they've just had to eat—or drink. Suddenly, they're focused and leaning forward in anticipation. Both eyes are open and gleaming. Of course for some organizations in some parts of the country, I say, "Selling is like dating." That gets one eye open.

There are a number of ways in which selling could be said to be like sex. Seduction and sales are often considered cousins. Okay, kissing cousins. And some salespeople do seduce their customers, sometimes seducing and abandoning them and moving on to the next conquest. Some salespeople dress themselves, their companies, and their products up in their best Sunday finery, primping and plucking, hiding imperfections with heavy makeup and flattering lighting. They make the sale. It's only after the seduction that the customer discovers the reality of the relationship: like the disappointed lover who finds that her slick-talking, smooth-walking, well-dressed seducer actually spends most of his time sitting around the house in a dirty T-shirt swilling beer, more interested in professional wrestling and Saturday afternoon naps than in paying attention to anyone else's needs, problems, or concerns.

The majority of salespeople, the overwhelming majority of us, are nothing like that. We want the best for our customers. And if we put the best face on our companies and our products and services, if we present them in the most flattering light we can find, that is, after all, our job, isn't it? Isn't that what everyone does when they're courting? And if there are one or two little things—small, less flattering details—that some of us never quite manage to find the perfect way to present during the courtship, well, there will be time enough to deal with those down the road, in the future, with any luck the distant future.

You can sell like that. You can be successful. You can, that is, if you're not concerned that the product or service you're selling is somewhat different from the one you'll be delivering. If you don't mind that what you're really selling is customer dissatisfaction. If you aren't trying to build the best possible long-term relationship with your customers. If you're not interested in growing old and happy and prosperous together.

Truth is after all the ultimate sales tool.

But none of that is why I tell audiences that selling is like sex. Selling is like sex because if you're not having fun, you're not doing it right.

Selling should be fun. Of course, just like sex, selling is a lot more fun if you don't have to worry about pretending to be something you're not. Hey, guess what? Sooner or later—probably sooner—your beloved is bound to figure out that you'd rather watch *Death and Guts III* than *Hearts and Rosebuds*. And what about that slightly unstable, not-really-homicidal ex-wife you've neglected to mention? You have two choices. You can present that unsettling little reality yourself—putting it in perspective as just a small part of the whole story—and be free to take the proper measures to deal with the issue. Or you can keep it secret and wait until your new girlfriend's pets start disappearing.

Fun Is a Sales Strategy

If you can make selling fun for yourself, you can make it fun for the prospect. If you can make it fun for the prospect, you're halfway to a sale. If laughter is the best medicine, it can also be the best salesmanship. This brings me to a customer comment that I quoted in that ancient evaluation of the ride-along with my top sales rep. The customer said, "I never laughed so much on a workday." And that laugher, that fun the rep was able to generate in those calls, had a great deal to do with why her prospects had the tolerance to give her eight nos without reaching for a shotgun. They were having fun!

Bragging about Your Own Negatives: My Sorry Butt

Obviously, you have to be careful with humor in a sales call. You don't want to offend anyone. That's why self-deprecating humor can be so powerful. You're poking fun at yourself. No one else is likely to be offended. It makes you seem modest and likable while at the same time demonstrating that you're confident and self-assured enough to laugh at your own foibles. In effect, you're bragging about your own negatives.

"So there's no question it's the right product for the right price," I once told a prospect.

"It's a great product. It's a good price."

"And this is certainly the right time." It was. And I'd given him any number of excellent reasons why.

"I'm still not convinced that I need to order right now, today," he said.

I nodded. "That's because I forgot to mention the best reason."

"Oh, and what's that?"

"Because that's the quickest way to get my sorry butt out of your building."

"Sold!"

That became known around the office as the *sorry butt* close. Not only did I use it again from time to time, but a couple of other reps started trying it as well. It worked just often enough that every new hire got to hear about Barry Maher's sorry butt.

A young entrepreneur once had a meeting with the top executive team of his number-one corporate client in the office of the CEO. Being a good salesperson, he was actively working at building rapport, especially with the CEO. But the man was a good

40 years his senior, and as the other executives stood listening in near silence, the small talk soon became miniature and then microscopic. Searching for clues to the man's interests, the entrepreneur hit upon that old standby, a photo prominently displayed on the huge desk.

"What a beautiful young lady," he enthused. "Is that your granddaughter?"

A stunned silence seized the room. The CEO shot him a look that could have frozen fire. "That, sir, is my wife," he muttered.

Now it was the entrepreneur who was stunned. All he could think about was all those sales, all that money—a huge percentage of his business—vanishing as quickly as the CEO's smile. He glanced around nervously. No one would meet his eye. But he happened to notice a ceremonial sword resting on a shelf on one wall. He rushed over, grabbed the sword, snatched it off the shelf, then dashed back and dropped down to his knees directly in front the CEO's desk. He bowed his head and slowly raised the sword high in from of him. Then, suddenly, he plunged it down . . . into the space between his arm and his body. He fell face down, twitched once or twice, gurgled a death rattle, and lay still.

Yet another stunned silence. Then the room erupted into laughter. After a moment, the entrepreneur peered up cautiously and saw that the CEO was laughing too—not as loudly as the others perhaps, but laughing nonetheless. The tension was broken. The account was saved.

Have fun with your job. Have fun with your prospects. As far as I'm concerned, he or she who has the most fun wins. Tattoo that on your arm. Just remember laughter is a two-edged sword. It works a lot better when it's pointed at yourself.

You also might remember that selling is like sex. If it's not good for both of you the first time, you might never get a second chance.

Management: Helping Your People Collect Their Nos

If you're in sales management or aspire to sales management, I offer this section as the world's shortest course on how to succeed as a sales manager. At least, it's about everything I know about how to succeed as a sales manager. So if you're thinking of hiring me as a management consultant, you might simply want to read through it and save yourself a small fortune. The section that follows contains everything I know about how *not* to be a sales manager. Nobody ever hires me to consult on that. Of course a lot of companies already have more than enough expertise on how not to manage.

I once took a position as a sales manager in a Fortune 100 company, having been told that my new team had been the number-one unit in the region the year before. When I reported for work, however, I found that the six-person unit had three new, foundering rookies and one opening, where the top salesperson in the entire division had recently transferred out. For the present year, the unit was dead last in the region and so far in the hole that, no matter how much they sold, some of them wouldn't see commission checks for at least 2 months. And because of the way the previous manager had manipulated the current sales canvas to ensure his promotion, each rep was stuck with a desk full of problem accounts, all of which had to be dealt with immediately. Morale would have had to improve greatly to reach abominable.

Within weeks my boss—the brand-new region manager—announced her retirement. Her replacement was instantly disliked, and everything he tried seemed to make the problem worse. He established what seemed like thousands of goals, most of them vague and some of them conflicting. He overpraised for slight accomplishments and never noticed significant triumphs and milestones. His "motivational" talks left veterans snickering and rookies confused.

In my first meeting with my new unit, I'd told them that within 1 year they were going to be the number-one unit in the region. Within less than a year, they were. So how did I build their morale and turn the team around?

I didn't. They did. I just did a few things to help make it possible. The program was simple:

1. **I demonstrated faith in them.** To me, leadership is not really about leading other people. It's about leading yourself, about having a clear path you honestly believe in to follow and the conviction to follow it. Beyond that, it's about showing your people that there is more in them than they know, so they'll be unwilling to settle for less.

   I made it clear to my reps that I truly believed that individually and collectively they had the capability to be the best. Then I acted as if that were true. Within a very short time, they were all trying to live up to my expectations. In a little while longer, they had adopted those expectations as their own, which meant they worked even harder to fulfill them. To succeed, people have to believe they can succeed.

2. **We set specifics goals and an ultimate goal.** Few of us have ever done anything to the best of our ability, to the limits of our potential. We set some very specific goals, but the challenge I made to my people was this: See how well you can perform if you perform as well as you possibly can. So each rep's ultimate goal was completely straightforward: simply to try to work to the best of his or her ability, to commit to doing the best possible job in every call, every day. Since that ultimate goal had no number attached to it, reps didn't slow down when running ahead of quota or slack off when falling behind.

3. **I demonstrated my loyalty to them.** I fought for them and championed them in the region and in the company. I always tried to keep their best interests at heart. I found out what their short-term and long-term career goals were, and together we worked out concrete plans for reaching those goals. I did my best never to ask them to do anything without making it clear what was in it for them. It wasn't long before they were doing things just for me and for the company.

4. **I worked for them.** I explained my belief that the company was, pure and simple, a sales organization. That made those who did the selling the most important people in the company and all the rest of us—the administrators, the sales managers, the VPs, and the CEO—sales

support. Then I acted on that belief and supported them in every way I could.

5. **I praised and rewarded them for their accomplishments and made sure the company did the same.**

6. **Together, we created a team mentality.** We were going to be number one, and we were going to help each other to ensure that we all made it together. We set up a mentoring program that went beyond the nearly constant training that I was doing as the sales manager. The team members made sure that no one who wanted or needed help was ever left alone with a problem.

7. **We made it okay to make a mistake or to fail.** I did all I could to overcome their fear of failure, their fear of giving their best and proving to themselves, to me, and to those around them that they didn't have the potential they all wanted to believe they had. I also realized that I could never help them overcome their fear of failure unless I could first overcome my own. If I were afraid of failure, they would be afraid of failure.

They learned to review every call, as well as every day, every week, and every month, always asking themselves what they could have done better. With all the preparation salespeople have to do, the very best preparation for making sales calls is . . . making sales calls. But after absorbing the lesson in each call, they learned to absolve themselves—leaving the mistakes behind—and move on to the next call.

8. **Whenever possible, we turned negatives into positives.** Of course.

9. **We had fun.** And we made having fun on the job and in the accounts a priority. We tried to create an atmosphere where everyone would look forward to going to work and look forward to making the calls. Before long, we had a number of our customers looking forward to our sales calls as well.

Other Butts

As a salesperson, a consultant, a speaker, and a trainer, I've hired, trained, and worked with sales managers at every level of management. The best of them have taught me most of whatever it is I know about sales. The worst have also been a learning experience. But while the best managers cover virtually every personality type imaginable, the worst—the very worst—seem to have a number of characteristics in common. With apologies to Steven Covey, I offer this completely unscientific compilation of those traits, *The Seven Habits of Highly Defective People*.

1. They rely on other people for their thinking. Whatever the idea of the moment happens to be, that's what they believe. They're not only up on all the latest clichés and buzzwords, they pride themselves on it.

2. No matter how much they may prattle on about openness, inclusiveness, innovative thinking, and tolerance, they insist upon conformity and obedience.

3. Like a cheap politician, they never miss an opportunity to talk about their leadership skills, figuring that if they proclaim that they're leaders frequently enough, someone might actually follow them. True leadership, on the other hand, means never having to tell someone you're a leader.

4. They believe their own BS. Or desperately try to.

5. They'd take credit for the sunrise if they thought they could get anyone to believe it. They're certain they're responsible for anything their people might accomplish, although failures, mistakes, and screwups are obviously someone else's fault.

6. They're sure their own successes are the result of their superiority and/or their favor in the eyes of God. Other people are lucky, started life with silver spoons hanging out of their mouths, or just butt kissed their way to the top.

7. On the subject of butts, in spite of all their constant claims to the contrary, their actions are guided by the one overriding commandment of their universe: To thine own butt be true. They cover theirs, whatever the cost, although the cost is usually borne by someone else.

15

Give It a Shot: Closing Made Simple

I was on stage recently, finishing a speech at an awards ceremony for about 400 salespeople. We were all in formal dress, and just as I was concluding, I noticed for the first time that I'd neglected to pull up the fly on my tuxedo pants. What was worse, the audience noticed me noticing it.

I quickly put on a face of comic surprise, and the audience roared. Then, as the laughter died down, I leaned against the lectern, nodded knowingly, and said, "Remember the strategies we've discussed this evening. Remember the tips and tactics. But above all remember that none of them mean a thing . . . if you don't remember to close."

With that, I thanked them and walked off the stage. I got a much greater ovation than a professional speaker who can't even remember to pull up his own fly deserves, and for the rest of the evening, people were discussing whether or not I'd planned the whole incident. Whenever they asked me, I just smiled.

Sitting here now writing these words—without my fly open—let me say the same thing to you that I said to that audience: Remember the strategies we've discussed in this book. Remember the tips and tactics. But also remember that none of them mean a thing—nor do any other sales strategies, tips, and tactics—if you don't remember to close.

And If You Tell Old Ben Franklin to Go Fly a Kite . . .

If you think the Ben Franklin close I mentioned earlier is silly, picture this. You're the prospect. The salesperson you're with has finished a strong presentation and answered both of your initial objections. Now he slides the contract over in front of you and pulls an expensive-looking fountain pen from his pocket.

"Just give me your okay at the bottom of the page," he says, handing you the pen. "The first order will arrive next week."

You take the pen. If someone hands us something, we usually take it. You turn to the contract, pen at the ready, but you hesitate, poised over the signature line. *It sounds like a good deal, but* . . .

Suddenly, the salesperson reaches over and snatches the pen out of your hand—snatches it rather rudely. What the heck?

Turning slightly away from you, he shakes the pen once and then twice. "Darn thing's been clogging on me all day, but that should do it," he says and hands it back. "Try it now."

Amazingly enough in that situation, many prospects do just that, trying the pen out, signing the contract they had hesitated over a moment before, distracted away from their hesitation by a supposedly balky pen.

Closing on the Negatives

There are hundreds, perhaps thousands, of different sales closes. They all work. At least they all work at one time or another. Obviously, when closing you do everything you can to create urgency. You use all the honest tools you can muster and all the options your company provides. You use your favorite assumptive closes, forced choices, whatever you like. But closing isn't some magical spell requiring just the right incantation. One of my most successful final closes is the simple phrase, "Give it a shot." When you've sold yourself, when you can make your skeletons dance and you sell the whole story, a simple request for the order is often all it takes. In reality the entire call is the close. At the end of your presentation, you're merely asking for what makes sense. (Or if you use an assumptive close, you're expecting what makes sense to happen.)

Whatever the actual close itself might be, I like to set it up with more dancing skeletons. I make my original recommendation, let's say, the finest Premier-level package. As we discussed earlier, I make the prospect want the Premier before ever mentioning the price. I make him want it, even if he thinks that it's going to be far too expensive. Then I give him the price, provide all the reasons it's worth every penny of that price, and move into my initial close.

Often that will be a summary close. Most summary closes entail listing all the benefits then, in one form or another asking for the order. "As we've agreed Mr. Customer, the new Jiff-o-Matic is the fastest, the easiest, the most cost-effective . . ." It won't surprise you that when I do a summary close, that summary includes a negative or two—or three—among all the positives on the list.

Sometimes the prospect closes right away. Not usually, but once in a while, he closes right away. If he doesn't, I keep selling until I'm sure he can't or won't be able to buy the *Premier*. Then I try just a bit more, even though I don't expect it to work. At that point, and not before, I cut back to my secondary recommendation, slowly, *selling the negatives*. "Well, if you really can't see your way clear to go with the *Premier*—and as I said, I think you should give it some very serious thought—but if you can't, we do have the *Marquis Level*. Now, the Marquis package is *not* going to . . ."

And I list all the things the Marquis level won't do, all the ways it falls short of the Premier level, stressing any features the prospect will be losing that he's indicated might be important. Then I say, "But what the Marquis will do . . .," and I detail the positives—perhaps just a tad grudgingly—again stressing the features most important to him and any additional advantages, even beyond saving money, gained by cutting back. Perhaps the Marquis package will take significantly less storage space, or it will give him a chance to try out the product or service without such a lengthy commitment.

So I've set up a forced choice between my original recommendation and my cutback recommendation. Often at this point, the prospect takes over the selling and sells himself away from those features the cutback doesn't offer, features he needed just a few moments before, trying to sell me into agreeing that the Marquis Level is really best for his situation. It's astonishing how quickly vital features become unimportant when a significant amount of money can be saved. And if there's a feature or two found only on the Premier level that's still important to him, often I can find a way to package it with the cutback recommendation—either for free or at a relatively small additional price—as a sweetener to clinch the deal.

If he isn't losing *any* vital features by cutting back—and I made him want the original recommendation enough—anyone who's breathing, and a few who aren't, should be able to close the sale.

Cutting Back, Not Cutting Your Throat

If necessary, a good salesperson can cut back three or four or more times before finally getting the sale. The mistake mediocre salespeople make is that they cut back too quickly or they fail to stress what's lost with each cutback.

"No way," the prospect says, shaking her head. "It may be a Premier package to you, to me it just looks overpriced. Way overpriced."

"Well, we've also got our Marquis package," the rep says quickly. "Not only is it our highest rated in terms of customer satisfaction, it's considerably less expensive than the Premier. Actually, it's probably the best deal we offer."

Then why was he just trying to foist the Premier on her? If he was any kind of salesperson at all, there must have been good reasons. He needs to make certain she knows what they were. Otherwise his original recommendation loses all credibility, which means he loses all credibility—and the sale.

When done correctly, closing by cutting back can sometimes be as easy as cashing a big commission check. You just tell your prospects what they lose by cutting back—along with all the benefits they don't lose and anything they gain—and let them sell themselves. This strategy also helps minimize buyer's remorse. After you walk out the door, the prospect is far less likely to start feeling like he was sold something he wouldn't have bought on his own. And he's far more likely to feel he got the package he needed, the one he wanted to buy rather than the more expensive one you were trying to sell.

The Ultimate Negative

Many reps see the commitment they'll be asking the prospect to make—the commitment to buy—as the ultimate negative. I've seen salespeople so frightened of even indirectly asking for that commitment that they could scarcely bring themselves to give the price of their recommendation. I've seen even more who were afraid of the details of the contract that bound that commitment.

Poor salespeople keep the contract out of sight as long as they possibly can. They know it's an intimidating document that can strike terror into the pure of heart. When they're finally forced to haul it out, they place it in front of the prospect so warily and so tentatively that any potential buyer might be tempted to listen carefully to make sure it isn't ticking. Some reps might even neglect to mention a few of the full-disclosure details the prospect not only has a right to know but needs to know: details that could create major problems when they come to light later. And the tap dance that mediocre salespeople go into if anyone should try reading through the agreement on his own would make Fred Astaire weak with envy.

Eventually though, our hero does manage to ask the potential buyer for his "John Henry." That's because he's been taught never to say the words *sign* or *signature,* and over the years John Hancock (who signed the Declaration of Independence "so large that old King George won't need his spectacles") has somehow been replaced by John Henry (a steel-driving man).

Not that it matters. John Henry; John Hancock; John, John, the piper's son—there's nothing on earth this guy could call it that would get the majority of prospects to affix their signature to this obviously perilous agglomeration of legalese.

On the other hand, depending on her type of business, an accomplished salesperson might well have the contract sitting in plain sight during part or all of her presentation. (For that matter, depending on the type of business and the stage of the relationship with the customer, there are reps who might even have the contract at least partially filled out. Do not try this at home— or during a cold call—if you don't know what you are doing.) By the time she's ready for it, the contract is already starting to look familiar to her prospect, and he's not at all uncomfortable when she directs his attention to it.

I knew one insurance agent who kept two large stacks of contracts sitting on her desk. The message was: "This is a routine form. It's no big deal. Clients sign a lot of these every day." Obviously, if there was anything tricky or deceptive in the document, she'd never be so open, even though that very openness increased the odds that the prospect would sign and greatly decreased the odds that he'd read it before he did.

Never be afraid to be strong in asking for the commitment. Never be afraid to be strong about the details of the deal. You're telling the potential buyer what he has to do and the terms he has to accept to take advantage of that wonderful offer you're recommending. If you've sold it to yourself, if you believe it's everything you claim it is, those terms are more than justified. They're part of the price, and like price or almost any other potential negative, you should be able to brag about them. Use the Skeleton Protocol.

As one of my first sales managers used to say, "If it's worth it, why do you have a problem selling any of the terms—or anything about it? If it's not worth it, why are you selling it at all?"

Silent Treatment II: The Sequel

As I mentioned earlier, after a well-trained salesperson asks a closing question ("Would you rather we deliver it to your home or to your office?"), he shuts up. The conventional wisdom here is embodied in the odious phrase, *whoever speaks next loses.*

Salespeople can relate to other salespeople. We know what they go through, and when I'm buying something myself, I try never to make the salesperson's job unnecessarily difficult. Still, if I've got one who's less than forthcoming, who's cynically and obnoxiously trying to manipulate me, after he asks his closing question and shuts up, I might just shut up too. I'll take a look at my watch—sometimes I even set the watch's timer—to see how long it takes before he says something. If he's a firm, well-trained disciple of the system, it could be a while. But if I get tired of waiting, I just get up and start to leave. He'll talk.

I guess that means I win.

Back when I was a sales rep myself, I can remember absolutely horrifying one sales trainer. I'd just started with the company, so I didn't have a track record there, and the trainer didn't know my background. Now every salesperson on earth realizes that you can sell for your entire lifetime and not begin to have all the answers. So I'm always anxious to learn whatever I can from whomever I can. But this particular sales trainer was a former elementary school teacher who had done a little selling but obviously knew far more about training than he ever knew about sales. The suggestions he'd offered so far that day had been ludicrously off the mark. And though I'd been polite, there was no way I could follow even a single suggestion, and he was becoming frustrated, especially since I was having an outstanding day. In four calls, I had four excellent sales, including one I closed after the trainer had actually stood up and started to pack our things, reciting, "Okay, so when would be a good time for Barry to come back for your answer? Would Tuesday at 10 A.M. be best or would you prefer Wednesday at 2?" I almost expected him to actually call the prospect Mr. Customer.

During the next call, he interrupted me and hijacked the conversation off in another direction just as I was about to move for a commitment. He had no idea how close he came to killing the sale, or how close I came to killing him.

After that call, he offered just one comment. He read it to me as he entered it into the notes on his clipboard: "A good day. Everyone wants to buy—*in spite* of the way Barry's selling. No doubt he'd be selling even more if he would learn to sell correctly." Obviously, I could expect a scathing evaluation. But the wonderful thing about sales is that you don't have to worry about anyone else's opinion. The results speak for themselves.

The final call of the day was on a corporate VP named Rudy Hastings. Rudy and I quickly developed a strong rapport, and based on my fact-finding I made a huge recommendation. It was completely justified, and I sold it hard—not high-pressure, just good-natured persistence. We had the same sense of humor so that persistence was accompanied by a lot of laughter. Still Rudy had never done business with our company, and I didn't expect to close him at that level. I was really just changing the scale, figuring that we'd negotiate down and still get him started with a good size initial order. The huge orders would come in the future.

I asked a closing question. I shut up as prescribed; there's a certain amount of truth behind the conventional wisdom. Waiting for Rudy's response, I studied his face. It was so expressive you could almost see his thoughts. Then, from the corner of my eye, I caught the trainer waving his hand at me. I glanced over—fortunately, Rudy didn't—and the trainer put a finger to lips and nodded, telling me to keep quiet: Whoever talks next loses.

Now normally, I wait after a closing question, but if an answer isn't forthcoming after a reasonable interval, I often jump in with a gentle nudge. Sometimes I repeat one or two of the strongest selling points. Sometime I just shift in my chair to draw the customer's attention, or tap the contract once with a finger, or move it just slightly closer to the prospect.

Then I say simply, "Give it a shot."

But this time, as soon as I got that signal to shut up, I cut the waiting short. "Rudy," I said, "buy the damn stuff. Give it a shot."

I glanced over at the sales trainer. He jaw was open in stunned disbelief. Then he snatched a pen from his pocket, raised his clipboard, and began to write furiously—so furiously he never noticed Rudy signing the largest contract of the year.

Why Wait? Cancel Now!

Buyer's remorse and customers recontacting and cutting or canceling orders can be big negatives—for the rep. But they can also be negatives for the customer. Certainly, there are times when after a bit of calm reflection, the customer realizes that he made a mistake and needs to reduce his order or cancel it altogether. But frequently, like a student on a multiple-choice test, the customer's initial decision is on target, then in an agony of buyer's remorse and second guessing, he jumps to a poor one. This is a phenomenon I'm intimately familiar with because as a consumer I'm practically the poster child for buyer's remorse. If Jerry Lewis held a Buyer's Remorse Telethon, he could probably do a good hour and a half on me.

An industrial solvent manufacturer had historically allowed customers to cancel orders right up until the goods were shipped. Eventually though, processing costs forced them to limit the cancellation period. To make certain there was no confusion about the new policy, the legal department came up with a new clause that reps had to handwrite across the top of the contract, just after it was signed. It read, "Contract May Be Canceled within Seven (7) Days." And of course the customer had to initial it. The reps hated the whole concept. Their old customers protested over the shortened period. New customers were alerted that what they thought was a binding order could be canceled anytime during the next week. Cancellations soared.

Reps tried every way they could to mealy-mouth around the dreaded clause and often ended up calling even more attention to it. A few reps became adept at the sleight of hand of getting people to initial the line without realizing what they were initialing, thus defeating the purpose of having it there in the first place.

The solution to the problem was just another form of making the skeleton dance. Much as I'd love to be able to claim it as my idea, the truth is it came from one of those lengthy brainstorming sessions where no one is ever quite sure who contributed what. I do remember that I paid for the pizza, so I should get credit for that much at least.

The upshot was that the company trained the salespeople to cover all the other pertinent terms of the contract and have the customer sign it. Then the rep would write out the 7-day clause and say, "I need you to initial this line right here. Obviously, it means that you can cancel the contract anytime within the next 7 days. But I'll tell you what: If you're going to make any changes, let's make them right now, while I'm here. That's a whole lot easier for everybody."

At least one sales manager thought he was going to get lynched when he first unveiled this strategy to his people. "You're soliciting buyer's remorse before you're even out of the call," one veteran complained. Someone else added, "You just got them to commit. You just closed them. Now you're reopening the decision all over again."

Yet another rep griped, "You're telling people they've got to back out right now or they're stuck. They're all going to back out. You're going to kill every single deal."

Fortunately, that's not what happened. Since the customer had already signed the contract, having the salesperson tell her that she had one last chance to make changes—basically "speak now or forever hold your peace"—reinforced the decision she had already made and got her to make the additional decision to leave everything as it was, not only then but in the time to come. And once again, it showed the rep to be trustworthy and confident. Cancellations were reduced to a minimum.

If buyer's remorse and customer recontacts are a big problem, it's better to bring the issue up yourself and deal with it— it's better to make that skeleton dance—than just pretend the problem doesn't exist and hope it doesn't happen.

"By law [or "company policy is"] you've got 72 hours to cancel. But if you're going to make changes, let's make them right now, while I'm here. It's a lot easier on everybody." And it is.

"How Can I Miss You When You Won't Go Away?"

Life to me is a lot like golf. No matter how much expertise I develop in an area, no matter how much I practice, no matter how ingrained the most effective ways of performing might become, from time to time I'm still capable of staggeringly brilliant flashes of ineptitude. No matter how good I get, once in a while I still blast a ball from a sand trap on one side of the green directly, on the fly, into a sand trap on the other side.

Selling is better than golf. And here's why.

Occasionally during my career as a sales rep—on far more occasions than I care to admit—I'd screw something up. A bogey loomed, perhaps a double, even a triple bogey. I'd be talking to Hank Dalrymple, and old Hank had a strong need for exactly what I was selling. In spite of that, a supposed hotshot like me hadn't been able to close him. Or maybe I'd closed him—so it looked like I'd done my job—but I'd undersold him. I'd settled for the easy, smaller sale—for whatever Hank might have been willing to buy—when I should have been stronger, better, more effective, and made the more expensive and therefore more difficult sale, and sold Hank what he really needed. And the more he needed it, the more it would bug me that I hadn't done my job.

I always analyzed each call after it was over, no matter how successful or unsuccessful, to try to figure out how I could have done it better. But on these calls I'd head back to the car shaking my head, usually knowing before I got the key in the ignition exactly what I should have done and wondering why on earth I hadn't done it.

Now a lot of salespeople would rather let vultures snack on their intestines than walk back into a call they've just left, especially if they've actually made a sale. But for me, it was easier to walk back in than to let a call like that eat at me for the rest of the day. Besides Hank needed the product. Providing customer service meant selling him what he needed, not what he might be willing to buy. So I'd take another minute to reevaluate my strategy and figure out exactly how I wanted to approach it. Then I'd march back into the call.

"Hank," I'd say, "I just had to come back here and apologize to you."

"Apologize?"

"It's completely my fault. You know, sometimes when you're in a hurry, when you've got appointments waiting . . . and sometimes when you're explaining something over and over to a lot of different people, well, once in a while you just don't do the kind of job that people have a right to expect."

That's the basic thrust of the walk back close. "Obviously," the salesperson says, "it's my fault you didn't buy as much as you should have. It's my fault for not explaining the product—the opportunity—better." In effect the rep is bragging about his incompetence, his failure. Obviously, a decent salesperson would have made it clear why Hank needed whatever it might be that he needed. But in good conscience the rep really can't leave things as they stand because there's just no question Hank really does need more than he purchased. There's no question at all for the following reasons . . .

The real power of the walk back close is that you are telling the truth. If you'd done a better job, Hank would have bought more.

When I had the right customer for a product that I truly believed in, I used to walk back into calls regularly. A huge percentage of those customers significantly increased their orders. And often, very often, people who'd refused to buy at all—who'd told me no any number of times just a few moments before—would buy on the walk back, and sometimes they'd buy big.

How Are Things in Ballyglunnin?

"So what's the best close?" novice salespeople frequently ask me.

"The Ballyglunnin," I always tell them. "Pull it off and it's not only the easiest close, but the customer will keep ordering for years to come. The problem is that you can't use the Ballyglunnin on the first sale. On that first sale, there are any number of ways you might close. Different salespeople prefer different closes, and what works well for me might not work nearly as well for you, and vice versa. But there is a single best way to close— not this sale—but the next sale. And that's to see that the current sale leads to a truly exceptional experience."

So what does that have to do with Ballyglunnin? Let me tell you why I can't wait to book my next vacation in Ireland.

Many of my father's fondest memories were of his early childhood in Ballyglunnin in County Galway, Ireland. He lived in a castle, he told us, and learned to love learning in a tiny one-room school. Castle or no castle, once in the states, his mother cleaned houses; his father was a laborer. Through their efforts, my father became the first Maher to complete high school and then college, at Notre Dame. I still have the letter he wrote his parents when he was accepted at Harvard Law School.

"From housecleaning to Harvard in a single generation," he'd say later. He loved America for that. Still, his life was hardly easy. He nearly died during World War II and lost a wife and two children within a year. Later, three other children would die. Those of us who reached adulthood did so with the best educations money could buy, and he raised a company president, two corporate vice presidents, a telecommunications executive, a doctor, and me. He always dreamed of returning to visit Ballyglunnin, but with all that educating to do, there was never the time and never the money.

The only time I ever saw my father cry was when we, his children, bought him that trip to Ireland for his 80th birthday. One of my sisters and I were looking forward to traveling with him, but unfortunately—though he'd been practicing law a few months earlier—his health deteriorated rapidly and senile dementia set in. Soon he didn't even recognize us. The trip never happened.

Then last year, for no discernible reason, my book *Filling the Glass* took off in Ireland, and I was booked on a speaking tour there. I was determined to visit Ballyglunnin, the castle, and the one-room school, but my schedule was tight.

Ireland has become one of the true economic success stories of our young century. The leading industry is of course tourism. The entire country has embraced the industry. The Irish have developed a reputation as the world's greatest hosts, a reputation that turned out to be actually true rather than just marketing hype. Even though I wasn't really a tourist, I was immersed in that hospitality. At engagements I was treated more like a guest than someone they were paying to speak. There were dinners and receptions and "must see" sights to be seen. All of this left me only one day for Ballyglunnin.

I set off for the tiny hamlet with several sets of complex directions and three conflicting maps. Every time I stopped and asked for directions, I was embraced like a long-lost relative, but though a few people had heard of Ballyglunnin, no one was quite sure where it was. I must have bounced along every back road in County Galway, but none of them led to Ballyglunnin.

The next morning, in Galway City, I spoke of my father during my final presentation, and I mentioned in passing what had happened the day before. At the luncheon afterward, I was finishing up my lasagna—which seems to be a particular Irish favorite—and thinking about heading upstairs to my room to pack. That's when the CEO announced, "Mr. Maher, your car has arrived, complete with the savviest driver in all of Ireland."

Less than 2 hours later, the limo, myself, the CEO, and a local Member of Parliament pulled into Ballyglunnin. The locals decided I was a returning hero and took us on a tour of the village, the old one-room schoolhouse, and the "castle"—an aging, rather modest resort hotel where my grandfather had run a small shop. But it was a castle indeed to any 7-year-old.

The real highlight of the trip came upon my return. Though my father hadn't recognized me in over a year, when I showed him my photos of the school and the "castle," his cloudy eyes slowly cleared. Then those eyes met mine. "Ireland," he said softly. "Thank you, Barry, for Ireland."

Thank the Irish for Ireland. That's the feeling you get when you travel through Ireland. It's not just customer service; it's that any number of people you meet seem to enjoy nothing more than going out of their way to make certain you enjoy every moment of your trip and get the most out of the country they seem to love so much. It took me 50 years to get to Ireland the first time. And it took a business trip to get me there. Now I can't wait to become a repeat customer on my own dime.

Truth: Truth is the ultimate sales tool.

And if the actual experience of doing business with you is everything you claim it will be and perhaps even more—and you insist on making sure that it is—the next sale will be the easiest job you'll ever have.

That's the Ballyglunnin close. And it's the close of this book. It's my hope that the anecdotes, the stories, the examples, the parables, and the pontifications you've found here will have conveyed a few truths and made the experience of doing business with me everything I'd like to claim it is.

That's my only chance of selling you a sequel.

Barry Maher
Las Vegas, NV/Helendale, CA
www.barrymaher.com

Index

Invoicing, delayed, 90
Ireland, 170-172

J
Jefferson, Bill, 43
Jordan, Michael, 143

K
Kean, Steve, 126

L
Land mines, treating negatives like,
 7-8
Laughter, 145
Leadership, 149, 153
Legitimate points, granting, 121,
 123-127
Lifetime guarantees, 42-46
Lincoln, Abraham, 39
Listening, 142
Long-distance telephone companies,
 5-7
Loyalty, 150

M
Making the skeleton dance, 3, 15-22
 with candor, 19-22
 impossibility of, 85-87, 95-96
 with more expensive, less reliable
  products, 16-19
 protocol for (see Skeleton
  Protocol)
 for yourself, 29-30, 85-87
Management, sales, 148-153
Manner, 107

Manson, Charlie, 39, 42
Mealy-mouthing, 8-11
Mentoring, 151
Miller, Henry, 34
Miss Texas beauty pageant, 21
Mistakes, 151
Modified limited cons, 13-15
More complete offers, 89-91
More expensive, less reliable
 products, 16-19, 57-61
More expensive products:
 making skeleton dance with,
  16-19, 57-61
 positive presentation of, 48-50

N
National Leadership Award, 13
Negative(s):
 acknowledging, 29, 33-35
 bragging about, 15-16 (See also
  Making the skeleton dance)
 in close, 158-159
 commitment to buy as, 160-162
 and conning customer, 11-13
 dealing with, 1-16
 finding positives in, 37-46
 focusing on, 37-38
 hiding, 4-7
 land mine approach to, 7-8
 with legitimate business reasons,
  49
 mealy-mouthing about, 8-11
 memorableness of denying, 126
 and modified limited cons, 13-15
 positive edge of, 39-40, 51-56

About the Author

Barry Maher is a cutting-edge consultant and an unforgettable speaker. His client list ranges from ABC/Capital Cities to the National Lottery of Ireland to Verizon (not to mention Ameritech, BellSouth, and SBC). And he's frequently featured in publications like *USA Today, The New York Times, Business Week, Success,* and *The Wall Street Journal,* as well as in *Sales and Marketing Management, Selling Power,* and *Sales and Marketing Insider.*